Governments of OECD Member countries are endeavouring to improve the efficiency and effectiveness of the public service. A major theme in reform initiatives is the need to develop more flexible and innovative approaches to personnel management which can contribute to increased productivity and support the drive for better management of public sector organisations.

This publication has been prepared by the OECD's Public Management Service. It brings together a series of papers on various aspects of flexible personnel management in the public sector, prepared for two meetings organised under the auspices of the Technical Co-operation Committee (now the Public Management Committee) in 1988. The papers, contributed by senior government officials responsible for personnel management and leading private sector analysts, provide insights into and analysis of public sector personnel management trends, issues and policies in a range of OECD countries. The Technical Co-operation Committee recommended that the report be made available to the public. It is published on the responsibility of the Secretary General.

Also available

ADMINISTRATION AS SERVICE: The Public as Client (1987)
(42 87 01 1) ISBN 92-64-12946-4 136 pages   £9.00   US$18.00   FF90   DM40

THE CONTROL AND MANAGEMENT OF GOVERNMENT EXPENDITURE (1987)
(42 87 02 1) ISBN 92-64-12995-2 188 pages   £13.00   US$27.00   FF130   DM56

STRATEGIES FOR CHANGE AND REFORM IN PUBLIC MANAGEMENT (1980)
240 pages.
Out of print. Available on microfiche.

Prices charged at the OECD Bookshop.

The OECD CATALOGUE OF PUBLICATIONS and supplements will be sent free of charge
on request addressed either to OECD Publications Service,
2, rue André-Pascal, 75775 PARIS CEDEX 16, or to the OECD Distributor in your country.

TABLE OF CONTENTS

INTRODUCTION

All OECD Member countries are actively seeking to improve the efficiency and effectiveness of their public administrations. One of the main characteristics of this activity is the pursuit of more dynamic, flexible, and varied administrative structures. This is seen as a necessary response to the increased complexity and scale of public sector policy–making, the need to create and sustain an effective partnership between the public and private sectors and the wish to improve the quality of public services and their responsiveness to the needs of citizens.

Given the pressure to limit public sector expenditures, administrative reform has often been initiated through changes in financial management; but countries have increasingly recognised that more varied, adaptable, and responsive structures can only be created through the support and active co–operation of public service officials themselves; that what amounts to a cultural change in the public service must begin with and be driven by innovative policies for the management of the human, as well as the financial, resources of the public service.

The Public Management Committee of OECD has therefore given high priority to exchanging information between Member countries concerning innovative developments in the management of human resources in the public service, and to the analysis of trends and issues in current personnel policies.

As part of this work, an informal meeting of experts on the subject of flexibility in public service personnel management was organised in early 1988 and a conference of OECD Member countries was held in late 1988. A selection of the papers contributed to these meetings are now being made generally available through this publication, as a contribution to the exchange of ideas and experience in this important and developing area.

The first paper, by *Sue Richards*, compares personnel management practices in the public and private sectors, on the basis of an examination of the civil service and the Post Office in the United Kingdom and the Shell Netherlands company. The paper concludes that greater decentralisation of personnel management is essential to the achievement of the flexibility which organisations require to function effectively in a rapidly changing environment. The public service must adopt more flexible rules, but within a "loose–tight" framework that combines a centrally determined strategy with a decentralised system of operational action.

The importance of establishing such a framework is also brought out in the paper by *Lennart Gustafsson*. His review of recent changes in pay and other personnel policies in the Swedish public service, points to the importance of more flexible, decentralised policies in making the public administration more efficient and service–oriented. He notes, however, that limits have been set to the extent of flexibility, whereby certain basic conditions of service are decided centrally and remain common to the whole public service.

Drawing on Norwegian experience, *Per Laegreid* also sees decentralisation and delegation as central aspects of a flexible personnel policy. He too proposes a general framework which provides room for local arrangements. Yet he argues that because of the inevitable tensions between a continuing need for some central control (over the global salary budget, or to prescribe public service values and ideals, for example) and the introduction of local freedom to manage resources so as to satisfy efficiency and productivity goals, public service personnel policy has to function in an unstable equilibrium and personnel officials have to learn to live with ambiguities in the implementation of policy.

A warning note about the difficulty of achieving a fully decentralised system is sounded by *L.J. Wijngaarden* who notes that despite forty years experience of a steady decentralisation of responsibility for personnel management, the Dutch public service is still introducing changes designed to reinforce the central co-ordinating framework, and to overcome the lack of preparedness of individual managers for their personnel management responsibilities.

Increasing the mobility of staff, particularly at managerial level, both within the public service and between the public and other sectors, is a key component of flexibility policy in most countries. Mobility is seen as a way of providing managers with the range of experience necessary to cope with the complexities of modern public administration, and also as providing for more flexible allocation of human resources in response to shifting priorities. The paper by the *Treasury Board Secretariat of Canada* describes how greater staff mobility has been achieved for the senior levels of the Canadian public service, and how this has been accompanied and promoted by improved management development programmes.

In her paper *Sachiko Ikari* notes that in Japan, internal mobility is the main element of flexibility in an otherwise relatively rigid personnel management system operated by an independent central agency. She notes, however, that although mobility has been effective in matching resources to shifting policy demands, it is no longer enough by itself to cope with the demands being borne by the public service. The recent introduction of a broader range of flexibility policies relating to recruitment and rewards for staff with specialist skills may now point the way for a more general introduction of flexible personnel management.

Mobility is also the theme of the paper by *Jean–Pierre Ronteix*. Drawing on the experience of senior officials in the French public service, he sets out the advantages and disadvantages of mobility — for the individuals concerned and for the service as a whole. He concludes that the advantages of a high degree of mobility among senior officials greatly outweigh the drawbacks. Nevertheless there is a noteworthy paradox in the simultaneous movement of senior public officials to top positions in the private sector, and of private sector management methods into public administration, which raises its question of whether it would be more advantageous for the State to find ways of retaining its senior managers.

Rosemary Oxer's paper reviews recent experience in the Australian public service in coping with surplus staff, following substantial reductions in the number of senior executive positions. The management of staff displaced through efficiency reforms is one of the most sensitive and difficult issues facing public services, particularly when the pursuit of flexibility is leading to a reduction in the high levels of job security traditionally offered in the public service. The Australian experience in dealing with surplus staff provides valuable lessons for all countries facing human problems arising from efforts to introduce radical reforms in public administration.

James O'Farrell also reviews experience in reducing the number of civil servants, this time in Ireland. He outlines the efforts made to provide early retirement and to redeploy staff, as additional measures reinforcing a total embargo on recruitment.

Finally *Colin Fudge* reviews the issues facing public service managers as they seek to implement the various elements of a policy of flexibility, and questions who benefits from such a policy. He concludes that the pressure to introduce greater flexibility will continue; and that countries would benefit from continuing international sharing of innovation and experience.

It is our hope that this publication will make a useful contribution to that sharing.

FLEXIBILITY IN PERSONNEL MANAGEMENT: SOME COMPARISONS BETWEEN THE PUBLIC AND PRIVATE SECTORS

Sue Richards*

Introduction

This Chapter will explore some of the issues in personnel management flexibility as they bear on organisations in the public and private sectors. Primary emphasis will be given to discovering what lessons the public sector, and especially the non–traded public sector, can learn from elsewhere. However, one conclusion will be that there is no single model to follow, and organisations in the public domain will have to develop their own synthesis. While it is possible to make some general statements about the two broad categories — public and private sector — there are also many differences within each category. They are not homogeneous entities. Much of the discussion will therefore centre on particular cases, but conclusions of general significance will be drawn where possible.

In the public sector, the object of interest will be the British Civil Service. In the private sector, examples will be drawn primarily from Shell Netherlands. The British Post Office will provide an intermediate category: it is still publicly owned, but has undergone significant change in the human resources area, and at least part of it is being prepared for privatisation. What all three organisations have in common is a long history which has created organisational cultures that are clearly identifiable. They are all large organisations undertaking tasks of considerable complexity and interdependence across a wide set of professional orientations, geographical locations and technological contexts. In some respects, therefore, they bear close comparison because of their similarities.

The differences are equally marked. The obvious difference is not so much in ownership: ownership of the means of production is only one factor in determining how an organisation works. Of possibly greater significance, certainly for the issues involved in flexible personnel management, is the degree of market orientation built

---

* Senior Research Fellow, London Business School.
Primary sources for this report consist of interviews with employees of the organisations mentioned, together with documentation provided by those organisations and others.

11

into the way the organisation works. Both the privately owned organisation, Shell Netherlands, and the publicly owned British Post Office are oriented towards selling services or products to customers. That is how they survive. Although parts of the Civil Service in Britain are being placed in a market setting, sometimes artificially created to simulate market forces where internal markets are being set up, the historical legacy and most of the current actual practice involves services responding to the resource allocation process which springs from the making of collective not individual market choices.

The other difference of significance relates to the self–image of the organisations, and particularly how far they interpret their past performance as success or failure. With Shell Netherlands, part of an extremely successful multinational group, there is no doubt that future personnel management needs are seen as an extension of current successful practice. The system produced people who were capable of steering the company through choppy waters in the past, and it is assumed that this can be repeated by following the same general principles in the future. While the product of Shell Netherlands may change, the management process has proved successful and can be continued, adapting it to altered circumstances as necessary.

The picture in the other two organisations is very different. In both there is a rejection of the legacy of the past. Change is required, but not change of the continuous, adaptive kind pursued by Shell. Discontinuous change, radical transformation, is sought by the Post Office, which is fast becoming a commercial service business. Under the influence of the Thatcher government, the Civil Service is also attempting a management revolution, although it faces the additional difficulty of having to devise appropriate managerial models to encompass its full range of tasks.

Why Flexibility?

The British Civil Service is not unusual in being bound by an elaborate set of rules governing conduct. Max Weber's classic bureaucratic organisational form, whether in the public or the private sector, necessarily involves detailed elaboration of how people within the organisation should behave. A contemporary organisational analyst has suggested that bureaucracies generate "role cultures", where everyone is required to do what their job description says, no more and no less, because to do either would be to harm the plan of how the system as a whole should work[1].

Although "bureaucracy" is often now used as a term of abuse, it is worth recalling that bureaucracies were created out of a recognition that modern society generated such complex tasks that they could be achieved only by individuals combining their efforts in a rational, ordered way. Specialisation of labour led to higher productivity as well as improving the capacity to deal with complexity, and thereby enabled human beings to increase their collective wealth. Bureaucracies are underpinned by the idea that the whole is worth more than the sum of its parts.

This belief has been fundamentally questioned in recent years by a market–based philosophy which maintains that the actual performance of bureaucracies over the years suggests that in their case the whole is worth less than the sum of its parts. In the private sector, there are many examples of bureaucracies which were extremely efficient at producing goods, but which failed to adapt to changes in the market place potentially threatening to the demand for their product. The British motor–cycle industry and the American car industry are cases in point[2]. Those bureaucracies failed to acknowledge the significance of change and therefore failed to adapt to it.

In the public sector, which by definition is shielded from market forces, the influence has been indirect; there has been a diffusion of ideas about management and organisation from the market sector. This is an intellectual process hastened, in Britain and elsewhere, by the espousal of "public choice" type philosophies by governments. While the private sector has been forced to adopt new non–bureaucratic organisational forms to survive in the market place, the public sector has been the subject of equally strong pressure to change from political leaders.

The bureaucratic model has its virtues in dealing with the complexity and inter–relatedness of the world, but its disadvantages in terms of a poor capacity to respond to change have called it into question. In addition, the cardinal bureaucratic principles of equity, consistency, equality before the rule, accountability and procedural propriety have all come to be seen by current political leaders, not only of the Right, as obstacles in the way of enhanced managerial performance by the public sector. To many the State had appeared in the 1970s as a millstone round the neck of the private sector, consuming an ever growing proportion of national wealth. Cuts in public expenditure were seen as a necessary corrective, and improving the performance of the public sector became a priority.

Moving away from the bureaucratic paradigm is not easy. A system driven by the requirement to achieve equity, consistency and the other bureaucratic virtues is not readily turned into one driven by efficiency and effectiveness criteria. In the British Civil Service, there were additional problems in that the senior officials had always seen themselves as policy and personal advisers to Ministers, rather than controllers of a management operation, whether driven by bureaucratic or market principles.

This analysis over–simplifies reality, yet it is arguable that disenchantment with bureaucratic forms of organisation, in private and public sectors, provides an essential setting for a consideration of flexibility in personnel management policy and practice. It is this setting which explains the pressure to move away from the universalistic, rule–bound, centralised personnel management systems characteristic of the public sector. Such universalistic systems are appropriate for the classic bureaucratic form, but not for a performance–oriented approach where flexibility is needed, so that practice can be adapted to meet changing circumstances. As systems of devolved management are introduced to improve managerial performance, there is pressure to give local budget holders some degree of scope for flexible personnel freedoms to match their other budgetary freedoms.

It is, however, important to stress that flexibility and the absence of a clear personnel strategy are not one and the same thing. Consideration should obviously be given to long–term needs in personnel policy, and also to how the different parts of a more flexible policy fit together, if necessary. A strategic approach is made more difficult in a centralised personnel management system by the need to concentrate on the administration of detail. Guarding the rule–book diverts attention from thinking about the larger questions. Flexibility and strategy go hand–in–hand, they are not negations of each other.

The Context of Flexibility

While the need for change is seen as the primary motivation for personnel management flexibility in the private and public sectors, it bears on these two areas rather differently. For companies like Shell Netherlands, the route between success in the past and in the future is characterised by continuity and development. The emphasis is on continuing the record of success. The company has demonstrated a responsiveness to the environment, and an ability to position itself so that it has security in the present, while preparing for change in the future. In the case of Shell, particularly, thinking about future scenarios is built into the way the company views the world.

For the British Civil Service, and other parts of the public sector such as the Post Office, change has been of a different order of magnitude. There may have been success in the past, but the present political regime has redefined past performance as failure. The route to success in the future is a discontinuous one, involving not just development from the present, but a quantum leap[3]. Paradoxically, whereas the private sector example covered has considerable expertise about using personnel strategies to stay at the level of excellence, the public sector has greater experience in the process of trying to get there.

Management change in the British Civil Service in the last ten years, since the Thatcher government was first elected, has been driven by two main factors, which have sometimes worked together to multiply the pressures to change, and at other times have tended to cancel each other out. The first factor is the government's desire to cut public expenditure as part of the strategy of rolling back the frontiers of the State, and the second is the quest for value for money, more efficient and effective management.

The pressure to reduce public expenditure has been unremitting, except for certain brief periods in the political cycle close to elections. The reduction has not been felt evenly across the board, so the pressures in some areas have been felt particularly keenly. Social infrastructure like housing, and until recently education and health, and the whole area of industrial support, have suffered, whereas defence and law and order have gained. These variations, however, mainly bear on programme expenditure. The pressure to reduce administrative expenditure has been virtually universal: approximately 70 per cent consists of staffing costs, and the attack on this area was signalled by setting a cuts target of 100 000 jobs, to be achieved by April 1984 and carried out successfully.

Anyone can make cuts if they do not mind loss of output, and that brings us to the second factor: value for money, and the improvement of management in government. The wasteful use of administrative expenditure was diagnosed as a major problem, and while the immediate round of cuts might eliminate excess in the immediate present, to improve management in the future required a major, discontinuous change. In addition to the introduction of better management systems, indeed as a forerunner, it was necessary to incorporate senior administrators in a managerial culture, a process still under way.

In order to persuade the higher Civil Service to take management seriously, instead of considering it an activity fit for the lower ranks, it was necessary to alter their way of seeing the world. In other words, to use a familiar management of change model, it was necessary to unfreeze the old culture[4]. The hostile attitude of the Thatcher government to the public sector performed this function. The next stage in the change process involved introducing new ideas and persuading the custodians of the old culture, top civil servants, to take on responsibility for management. Finally, these new management ideas had to be applied systematically across the organisation. The Financial Management Initiative (FMI) fulfilled this requirement.

The Financial Management Initiative is based on the principles of accountable management, and although initially its significance for personnel management was not widely appreciated, it has become clear as the new systems have become more firmly embedded that it is not the systems themselves, but how people operate them, that matters. As a consequence, important personnel management policies have emerged rather later, and are only now catching up with the new systems. The drive towards improved performance has focused attention particularly on the need to recognise that Civil Service employees form part of the wider labour market. The recruitment and retention of key staff, and conversely the need to keep pay in certain economically depressed geographical areas in line with the local labour market, has been a crucial underlying factor in the belated attention being given to personnel matters.

Linked with these shifts in policy has been a consistent "deprivileging" of the Civil Service trade unions. Prime Minister Thatcher practised first on her own employees the approach to industrial relations which she was later to use in the wider labour market. A determined policy of detaching Civil Service pay from its private sector comparators, and then ensuring that settlements were made annually at low levels, has placed great strain on the old Civil Service union practice of negotiating universal terms and conditions. Whereas in the past those in a weaker position were strengthened through linkage with stronger brothers, this unity now seems to be breaking down. Pay agreements have been reached which contain performance elements and *de facto* market links for particular groups of staff which are clearly destined to overturn unified pay bargaining. This process is being accelerated by the creation of executive agencies, designed to tailor the management processes of particular parts of the Civil Service more closely to the needs of the task at hand.

The British Post Office has been undergoing what may be an even more radical transformation during the last few years. During the 1970s, its financial performance suffered as it was hit by both industrial strife and price restrictions. The future looked bleak, as the market environment started to become more competitive. A new chairman was appointed at the end of 1980, a former senior civil servant who was unusual in having had both contact with the private sector and also significant management training. Under his leadership, a change process was launched to adapt the Post Office to survive in a competitive environment.

It was recognised that the Post Office contained several different kinds of operation, each with its own competitors, and that to concentrate strategic attention appropriately it was necessary to decentralise into market–related units — or businesses, as they became known. A corporate board was to remain to manage interdependence between the units, but the four businesses — Royal Mail Letters, Parcels, Counters and Giro (the Post Office's bank) — would in future be the driving force for change. In order to increase the pace of change, considerable numbers of new managers were imported into the organisation, especially in functional areas previously only weakly represented, such as marketing and finance. As the new decentralised structure took shape, there was a similar decentralisation of the personnel function, with the onus for change moving from the corporate centre to the businesses.

Flexibility in Personnel Management — Some Comparisons

The previous section provides the necessary context for understanding the moves that have been made to increase flexibility. This section will describe the main features of the policies of increased flexibility. Particular attention will be focused on the attempts to import private sector practices, and an awareness of how the private sector works, into the public sector. This emphasis has been chosen not from a belief that the private sector has all the answers to the problems facing the public sector, but because that belief has underpinned much of the political pressure for change in the organisations discussed. The list of issues covered includes management development and training, appraisal systems and performance pay, recruitment and career development, and links between the organisation and its environment (for example through secondments).

Management Development and Training

The Financial Management Initiative had been under way for some time in the British Civil Service before it was acknowledged that accountable management, on its own, would not transform the organisational culture. A number of reviews were conducted at the centre of British government to investigate aspects of personnel management and they generated some change[5]. One significant change was the establishment of the Top Management Programme (TMP), a more or less compulsory six–week training course for new Grade 3s/Under–secretaries, generally thought to be the point of entry to top management. Four of the six weeks are spent with senior managers from the private sector. One of the objectives of the programme is to develop in civil servants understanding of the attitudes, priorities and approaches to major problems and issues which exist outside the Civil Service. The pursuit of this objective led to the most significant feature of the programme: the mixing of participants from public and private sectors for the four–week core course. Non–Civil Service participants are drawn primarily from big companies, although occasionally a participant comes from the voluntary sector, the health service or a local authority. Together they tackle case–study problems and thereby learn how minds work on the other side of the public/private divide. During this programme, friendships are often established which continue afterwards. The TMP has generated a network of contacts between the Civil Service and the private sector which had previously been very patchy in the fragmented elite structure of British society. It has contributed to the creation of overlaps between separate elites that has its most immediate significance in facilitating a change of attitude to management among civil servants, but in the long run may have wider impacts on policy.

The other major innovation is the Senior Management Development Programme (SMDP), which is designed to improve the training and career development of the next generation of top managers. This programme, like the TMP, signifies the end of the view that the only valuable form of knowledge was that acquired within the old culture. It is an acknowledgement that in the past the career development of future top managers was ill–suited to producing the right kind of person. It also involved a commitment to expanding tenfold the time spent by this key group in formal training — another sign of recognition that new skills were needed in the organisation. It has been difficult in practice to ensure that training targets were met because there is increasing short–term pressure on such people. Their peers are leaving the Civil Service in greater numbers than before, so those who are left behind have to fill the gap and cannot be spared from their desks. It seems likely that as civil servants improve their management skills through the SMDP they will become an even more attractive proposition to the private sector, a paradoxical situation.

Shell Netherlands and the Post Office have not given such high priority to management development policies that create links with their environment. For Shell

Netherlands, development emerges naturally from the coherent career planning discussed below. The marking out of those who are likely to go to the very top, and who will in the future be making strategic decisions that require a broad perspective, allows management development to be incorporated into their careers as they progress. Training and wider developmental opportunities are taken up when possible, between career postings, from a variety of sources, including Shell International, various business schools and others.

The Post Office has a number of in–house management training colleges, but these are aimed primarily at middle and junior managers, rather than at potential top managers. Recent recruitment policies have anyway introduced many external frames of reference into the thinking of the Post Office. In addition, the pace of organisational change since 1983 has been so rapid that management development policies, which are concerned with longer term issues, have not really been on the agenda. It has been all the personnel management function could do to try to acquire the skills needed here and now. For the moment, tomorrow has had to take care of itself. However, significant management development issues involving the "ownership" of key staff are likely to arise in the future. The corporate centre has a responsibility for long–term management development of the best operational managers, but the businesses need those good people to help improve performance today. The Post Office may have something to learn from Shell about how those dilemmas can be resolved.

Appraisal Systems and Performance Pay

The Civil Service has had an elaborate system of appraisal for many years, involving annual reports on all staff made by their line managers and then reviewed in turn by the line manager above. The appraisal form concentrated on the personal qualities demonstrated during the year by the individual, and the emphasis was on promotability rather than on performance in the present job. This assessment was a key factor in the progress of an individual to the next grade in the hierarchy.

Changes were recommended by a personnel review to link in with the development of management systems in the FMI, and a change of emphasis, laying increasing stress on performance in the job, was incorporated[6]. Now an official and the line manager agree the objectives for the year ahead, and the official is appraised in terms of the achievement of objectives. Nevertheless, it should be noted that not all objectives are capable of being measured precisely in the Civil Service environment. In advisory, regulatory and personal assistance roles, for example, the assessment of the impact an individual makes will still be a question of judgement rather than of measurement.

Ultimately, however, all appraisal systems rest on judgement, and the search for an objective system is in vain. In spite of improvements to the system made in recent years, it is still the same stock of human talent that is being appraised and, perhaps more importantly, doing the appraisal. We are again faced here with the fact that it is easier to continue to run an already good system, making minor improvements, than it is to achieve fundamental change. Lessons from the appraisal system in Shell Netherlands seem appropriate here. On paper, the system at Shell Netherlands does not look very different from the new Civil Service system, but the personnel practice lying behind it is of a different qualitative order. Although the same annual system of reporting applies, behind the system at Shell is a great deal of discussion, with the personnel function intervening to ensure that the judgements made on individuals in terms of

17

their current performance and their ultimate promotability reflect both a full range of considerations and, most importantly, are located within a consistent organisational framework, so that appraised individuals can be compared. There is a sense of strategic responsibility resting with the functional leaders for shaping the present and the future of human resources in the company.

In the Civil Service, the personnel function has rarely adopted a strategic focus. Most people in personnel jobs have no professional qualifications, and most will not have specialised in personnel through their careers. This is a recognised weakness in the system and efforts are supposedly being made to remedy it through an informal specialisation process involving several personnel postings in a career, although it is necessary for functional specialists to understand the organisation they serve and so they must also spend some time outside the function. However, the speed of this professionalisation process is so slow as to be almost imperceptible. In any case, in an organisational culture where professional qualifications are not highly regarded, professionalisation may not be the way to raise the status of personnel work.

Improvements in personnel practice fall victim to a lack of regard for the "people" side of management, in the present government and among some senior civil servants. Evidence for this view is seen in the progressive weakening of the leadership of the personnel function at the centre of government, with the abolition first of the Civil Service Department in 1981, and then of its successor, the Management and Personnel Office. There is a mistaken belief in those quarters that the private sector gets on with making profits, without giving time to think about the "soft" aspects relating to people. It is also the case in Shell that senior personnel managers have experience outside the function, but there is a tradition of professional competence which stretches back over the years. Shell could not be further away from the private sector stereotype. Personnel management there is regarded as an essential component in the past and future success of the company.

It is worthy of note that the British Post Office, like the Civil Service, has also been attempting to transform itself, in this case from a fairly bureaucratic public corporation (and until 1969, a government department) to a dynamic service business. Although still publicly owned, it aims to compete in its various markets with the best private sector competitors. Even where it provides a monopoly service, generic competition ensures that market pressures apply. Part of the strategy for transformation involved recruiting specialist skills from outside the organisation. As in the Civil Service, of which it used to be part, the notion of the generalist had prevailed. People were employed in a grade, rather than for a particular job, and it was assumed that if you chose the right people, they could turn their hand to anything. The prescription for transformation included abandoning the generalist culture and building up functional specialisms, so that people with relevant experience and training would be in a position to contribute to improved performance. Since pace is vital in organisational transformation, it will not happen at all unless it happens with speed, relevant skills had to be bought in from outside rather than developed in–house. This was done across the board; in marketing, accounting, engineering, transport management, and in personnel. As in Shell Netherlands, the quality of the personnel management function, especially in the Post Office's new market–oriented businesses, was seen as a vital ingredient in success[7].

Appraisal has taken on added importance in the Civil Service because of the introduction of performance–related pay. The Civil Service first entered this arena in

1985 with a performance bonus scheme. However, its introduction was ill–prepared, criteria for awarding the bonus were unclear, a percentage quota was imposed to limit costs to a given percentage of the total wage bill, and it was limited to certain middle management grades. Since that time, some of the lessons of experience have been learned, and new schemes are developing which are clearly linked to performance appraisal.

Flexibility in pay has moved a considerable distance in the last couple of years from the old universalistic system. The bridgehead was established in an agreement between the Civil Service and the trade union which negotiates on behalf of specialist staff. A complex arrangement of pay "spines" and "spans" allows the system to re-spond to crucial shortages in the supply of specialist labour, especially in the informa-tion technology market, by moving in principle towards market–related pay, although actual rates are failing to keep up with this fast–moving market, and performance–related pay. The bridgehead has recently been reinforced by expanding this agree-ment to cover tax collection specialists and, more importantly, senior middle managers (Grades 5 to 7). The most talented members of this group are the people most in demand from the private sector. Most are located in London where the cost of living, particularly housing, is high and where high pay in the financial and business services sector provides a great temptation to leave the Civil Service. Performance–related elements in pay are effectively permanent, so consistent high performers can move a considerable distance from the average, which until recently was what everyone was paid. After a sluggish start, the Treasury (the department responsible) has moved surprisingly fast and far on this issue, partly because there is a belief that market–related pay would lower the total wage bill. The most recent move on the pay front has been to extend performance pay right down the grade scale. In addition, one or two experimental schemes are being developed, such as in the Vehicle Inspectorate Execu-tive Agency, where group bonuses are being awarded for good group performance. The move to performance pay may not necessarily do much to improve motivation, but it does put pressure on to upgrade the quality of appraisal since immediate financial consequences flow from appraisal decisions.

Post Office managers also have a performance–related element in their pay, al-though there is more flexibility here as to the level of basic pay. Middle managers and above now have personal contracts which reflect recruitment and retention realities, rather than organisation–wide agreements. The criteria for awarding the performance element is manipulated to reflect current priorities in the business, and it is based on the achievement of measurable objectives, which is strongly reflected in the appraisal system. For example, in 1987, a certain proportion of performance pay was allocated to reward improvements in the quality of service in the Post Office Letters Business, to reflect this strategic objective.

If the Post Office is located at some distance from the Civil Service model, Shell Netherlands is further removed again. It is worth noting, however, that performance–related pay plays only a small part in the motivational assumptions that management makes. The quality of the appraisal system comes into play again here. People are recruited at graduate, and sub–graduate, level only if they are assessed as having the potential to reach senior management positions. Their progress, particularly in the early years, is comprehensively studied. It is assumed that the potential satisfaction, psychological and financial, of a successful career in Shell is a sufficient motivator on its own. If it is not, then people are encouraged to leave rather than being offered a bonus to revive their flagging ambition. This policy fits in with the research on per-formance–related pay, which suggests that in practice people are not motivated by pay when they have achieved what they see as a good basic standard. This is another case of sophisticated private sector practice being rather different from the crude stereotype held by some public sector management decision–makers.

Recruitment and Career Development

For all three of the organisations being considered here, future managers have been recruited primarily when people are in their early twenties, either as new gradu-ates or as promising school leavers. In the Civil Service and in Shell Netherlands, there has been a policy of recruiting high–quality graduates who were considered to have potential to rise to senior levels in the organisation. Both use a fairly elaborate system to assess potential, and both lay stress on the importance of intellectual ability as an indicator of future capacity to handle complex strategic issues.

The differences between the two begin to emerge in the process of selection. In view of earlier comments about the relative significance allocated to the professional personnel function as part of human resources strategy, it should come as no surprise that this difference of orientation is also reflected in the approach to recruitment.

The origins of the modern Civil Service are reflected very clearly in present–day selection procedures. In the nineteenth century, the major problem to be solved in this area was the high degree of nepotism in appointments, and the consequent poor quality of the civil servants recruited. In order to solve that problem, recruitment was allocated to a separate agency, with statutory independence to carry out its functions in its own way. Recruitment, a key element in any personnel strategy, is seen as standing outside the control of the senior personnel managers in departments. While they feed in their requirements to this agency, the Civil Service Commission, they nonetheless carry no responsibility for recruitment and it therefore exists on the margins of their concerns, although their lives are made much more difficult by the failure to select enough of the right quality of people, as has occurred recently.

The Civil Service Commission developed a recruitment process that enshrined the principle of merit, but like all such principles it was defined in a way that reflected the culture of the organisation and of the wider society. In particular, it involved a process of senior peer review which incorporated the assumptions of the old culture into the recruitment process. "Like recruits like" is an old personnel management aphorism, and it is amplified in the Civil Service, since the distanced relationship between the Commission and the rest of the personnel function in the service has made it difficult to reflect the new managerial orientation in recruitment. All recruitment above basic levels must be done at present through the Civil Service Commission, or under specific licence granted by them. Although recruitment covers many specialist fields, potential managers are considered to be a single category, whatever the nature of the opera-tional task of their department. A recent report, "The Next Steps", drew attention to the way in which the personnel management process in trying to suit the organisation as a whole, fits no one part of it at all well[8]. It has recently been decided to remove monopoly recruitment rights for the vast majority of civil servants from the Civil Serv-ice Commission. As of 1991, apart from a few fast–stream staff, departments will be able to make their own recruitment arrangements. They may use the Commission as an agent, or else use other providers in the market place or their own in–house resources.

The contrast with Shell Netherlands is quite marked. Recruitment is a core activity for the personnel function, and not hived off to some separate body — it would indeed be surprising if any organisation which did not share the Civil Service's particular history had adopted the same system. A further difference, however, is more significant. Shell requires long–term potential for the integrative role of general manager in its graduate recruits, but it recruits them for the first part of their careers to a particular function, or business. Shell Netherlands, itself a subsidiary of Shell International, is a holding company for a number of further subsidiaries, some of which are businesses, such as the exploration company, and some of which are functions, such as finance. Recruits spend the first years of their careers in these subsidiaries, to be moved on later to develop integrative capacities.

In developing firm specialist skills and experience first, before the general management capacities that the larger company needs, Shell may appear more inflexible than the Civil Service, which seeks generalist skills from the beginning. This is paradoxical, given the general line of argument about Shell's greater flexibility, but the answer to the conundrum lies in semantics, since the skills which the Civil Service calls "generalist" are a particular kind of specialism, rather than the integrative capacities that the term "general management" implies. "Generalist" should be taken to mean "specialist in the tasks valued within the administrative culture", tasks such as political support to Ministers, and presentational and representational tasks.

The contrasting approach in Shell to recruitment has an impact on the early stages of career development. The personnel function takes responsibility for its recruitment decisions by monitoring early performance thoroughly, so that those who get through the recruitment process but turn out not to be suitable in practice, as inevitably a proportion will do, are discovered and eased out before either party has made too much of an investment in the relationship. The Civil Service, by contrast, has made little use of the probationary period. The Administration Trainee scheme, which recruits graduates to a fast track career with accelerated promotion, requires a decision about a recruit's future career after two years. Only rarely are people "mainstreamed" — put on the decelerated track — or dismissed at this stage, implying either an improbably perfect recruitment process or a non–strategic, reactive exercise of the personnel function.

The "hands–off" approach in the Civil Service is continued in the field of promotion and posting. To qualify for promotion, managers must be in the "field" (which requires a certain number of years in the grade since the last promotion) and a certain number of annual appraisal reports marking them as suitable for promotion. Usually the next stage involves a promotion board, a committee with a personnel function representative and a number of others who come from other areas of line management. They meet to consider who among those eligible should be given promotion to the higher grade, either on the basis of interviews or simply an examination of the records. Once again the principle of peer involvement is enshrined in practice, and this has the predictable consequences of renewing the existing culture, rather than introducing change. Just as "like recruits like", so "like promotes like". In spite of all the words spoken about the importance of management in the Civil Service, the recent report could still legitimately claim that "the golden route to the top" involves being good at "old culture" administrative work[9].

Posting is also usually done in a reactive way. Personnel managers in the Civil Service do not have high status, and others with higher status, particularly Ministers, are able to make short–term demands which the personnel function is not equipped to resist. Ministers demand a better managed service, but — being political animals — they also demand the most able staff for their personal support and in high profile jobs. This means that carefully laid plans to develop an official's career in a particular direction can easily come to grief, experience which convinces personnel people that it is not worth trying to adopt a more strategic approach. In a more managerial culture, the personnel function would have more organisational authority.

Again, Shell Netherlands demonstrates that proposition. A pro–active stance is taken in career development, and an elaborate system of succession planning is in place, bringing together the immediate needs of the organisation and the developmental and personal needs of the individual. The relationship between Shell Netherlands and its subsidiaries demands a particularly pro–active approach, since it is in the interest of the subsidiary to retain good staff, for fear of damaging short–term performance. Nonetheless, the status of the corporate personnel function, together with the fact that a manager must make such a move if his career is to progress, ensures compliance.

Succession planning ensures that those who are likely to reach career plateaux at different levels have the appropriate mix of experience. This careful shaping of the company's human resources is regarded as a normal part of life, and acknowledged as a factor in success, past, present and future.

Links with the Outside World

The policy of seconding officials out of the Civil Service, to give them experience of the world outside, is being implemented with increasing frequency, although it still constitutes only a small fraction of the total numbers in Civil Service management positions.

Secondment is a classic illustration of the trade–offs between long– and short–term factors in personnel management. The greater vision that outside experience gives is of immense value, especially to an organisation that is trying to achieve major change in its culture. But the very people who could easily be seconded are the last people who can be spared in the short term. They are the ones wanted for ministerial support positions, legislative Bill teams, or special tasks of various kinds. This pressure to retain such people is increased by the exit of significant, if unrevealed, numbers of their peers from the Civil Service, many of whom have used secondment in the past as a route out of the organisation. In that context, and with all that has already been said about the non–strategic level of much personnel management in the Civil Service, it is perhaps surprising that secondment has increased as much as it has.

Two further aspects of current policy should be mentioned in this context. Many senior civil servants occupy *ex–officio* non–executive directorships in private sector companies, thereby increasing their knowledge of how the private sector works, as well as contributing an understanding of the Civil Service. A more recent move in the other direction has been the attempt by Lord Young, then Secretary of State for Trade and Industry, to incorporate private sector expertise within the policy–making process in his department, as part of the strategy for creating an enterprise culture.

What we see here is a determined attempt, despite the obvious difficulties, to create links, and even interpenetration, between the public and private sectors, this being part of a wider economic ideology and strategy. The other two organisations acquire their understanding of the outside world in other ways, mainly through the course of normal business, which in both cases involves interaction in the market place. The Post Office has boosted its understanding by importing managers in significant numbers. Shell Netherlands' highest flyers become part of Shell International, and there become involved in strategic scanning and planning which places knowledge of the market, and analysis of its environment, at the heart of organisational activities.

Conclusions

It was suggested above that flexibility in personnel management, and in other organisational functions for that matter, was important because it was a feature of the move away from the bureaucratic organisational form. While bureaucracies, in public and private sectors, had been responsible for achievements of great significance in the modern world, they had shown themselves to be insufficiently responsive to the need to change, and insufficiently motivated to achieve improved managerial performance. The world today is characterised by change of a discontinuous kind, involving radical breaks with the past in several aspects of organisational life. The most obvious example is the rapid rate of technological innovation, particularly in the field of information technology, where radical transformations can happen within the space of a few years. Economic, political and social changes happen almost as fast. The bureaucratic model for organisations — designed in a past era when it seemed more possible to plan in a rational way because responding to change was a question of extrapolating in a relatively ordered way from the past — is ill–equipped to deal with rapid change in the new turbulent organisational environment. Bureaucracies have a tendency to screen out and ignore messages which conflict with the dominant framework of opinion within them. They reject radical thoughts.

It is to enable large organisations better to respond to change that the call has been made recently to decentralise as much as possible of organisational decision–making. Partly this springs from influential private sector beliefs in the importance of being close to the customer. In most public bureaucracies, the least well–regarded people in the organisation, those at the bottom of the hierarchy, are the ones closest to the organisation's customers. They are the people who know most about the customer environment, but they are also the people whose voices are least likely to be heard in decision–making circles. (Even in a trading organisation, it is possible for the interest of the customer to be muffled by other interests. There may be professional interests, for example, which pursue technical innovation that will enhance professional reputations rather than wider organisational interests.)

Flexibility involves reducing the extent to which centrally determined rules govern decision–making, but it is not the same thing as abdication. To remove the controls and let the organisation succeed or fail would be to abdicate strategic responsibility for the future of the organisation. Flexibility can only come from a strategic approach, from coherent decisions about what does and does not need to be decided centrally, and what can be left to the discretion of others in the organisation. It requires a recognition from those at the centre that action to preserve uniformity may damage managerial performance, and therefore should be taken only when in the utmost need. In the cases examined here, the level of strategic capability in the personnel management function differs markedly. In Shell Netherlands, the personnel function seems to be at the heart of organisational decision–making. A successful organisation attributes its past success partly to the way it deals with its people: the primary concern of the personnel function is to make sure that, just as in the past, there will continue to be a supply of top managers who have been through the right developmental process for Shell. Clearly, Shell believes that it has the right process for producing the right kind of people. While those people will make decisions as time goes by to vary the product — to divest in some areas of the multi–national's holdings, and to invest in new fields — the management process, by which the organisation renews itself, is seen to be right. Flexibility in Shell is in the area of production, and is facilitated by coherent strategic personnel management. The people developed through the personnel management process supply the organisation with its necessary flexibility.

The other two cases are quite different. Both the Post Office and the Civil Service are seeking not to continue the record of past success but to bring about organisational transformation and build anew the capabilities for future success. The Post Office has a clear commercial model in mind. Its future is clearly mapped out as a corporate group of service businesses. People in the Post Office now believe that only by successfully competing in an increasingly active market can they ensure that they will survive and prosper. Although some of its functions are concerned with a publicly owned monopoly service, which may well continue in such a form, it is believed in the organisation that the survival of that monopoly in the future rests on providing the service so as to respond to generic competition. (While there is a monopoly of the carriage of addressed mail with a stamp value of £1 or less, there are other ways of delivering messages which customers may choose if they do not get the service they need). The exercise of the personnel function has had to change radically to allow this transformation to take place. To introduce market–driven, commercial approaches within a predominantly bureaucratic, rule–bound structure has not been a simple task. The task has been achieved in the management field, where there has clearly been a major reorientation, aided by the decision to buy in from the world outside people with different skills and experience.

The transformation of the management approach, now that it has more or less been achieved, seems a minor problem compared with the industrial relations issues that remain to be resolved. Like many public utilities, the Post Office has been the home for a well–organised set of trade unions, which have used their strategic position over the years to defend their members' interests as they interpreted them. The changing industrial relations climate in Britain, as a direct and indirect result of government policy, has been very favourable to the Post Office management. Their approach has been to encourage the unions to participate in a "high productivity/high reward" framework, but so far this strategy has met with only limited success. In the area that is the primary focus, however, personnel management of managerial grades, success has been more marked. A coherent personnel strategy that has shaken off universalistic rules has provided the flexibility to improve performance.

The Civil Service faced more serious strategic problems in personnel management, and it still has furthest to go to achieve flexibility. The explanation for this lies in the nature of public management itself. Although the Post Office is still publicly owned, it has decided to act as though it were not, in that it has adopted a commercial, trading model. In such a case, and in the true commercial sector, the crucial transaction in the organisation is the sales contract, whereby customer and service provider exchange money and services. In the non–traded part of the public sector, the crucial transactions concern central resource allocation, which determines the resourcing of the service in question. Resource allocation springs directly from collective choices made by the public as a collective whole, and expressed through elected governments, rather than as individual customers[10]. That is the ultimate guiding principle of the non—traded area. Decision—making power is located at the centre of such organisations because that is where resources originate. The key transactions are between service providers and resource allocators.

It is in the context of that general principle that we must understand the present moves in Britain to achieve better value for money in government. Only through decentralisation, and a personnel strategy of increasing the flexibility of the rules governing management, can value for money be fully realised. Only by removing the detailed rules constituting the way that the centre has governed the periphery in the bureaucratic past can responsiveness and improvement—seeking behaviour be motivated. Yet the centre fears that to lose control of the detail would be to marginalise its position in decision—making, and to abdicate from its strategic role.

Perhaps the answer to this problem lies in re—conceptualising the centralisation/decentralisation dichotomy. "Loose/tight" properties have been advocated in a trading/market context to suggest that there are some things the centre should influence, primarily the organisation's culture, and some things that it should not try to influence, such as the detail of organisational action[11].

The Civil Service, whether it is acknowledged or not, is actually trying to tread new ground in management change at the present time. It is attempting radical organisational transformation, not simply to move from one paradigm to another, which is what the Post Office is attempting, but to create a new model that mixes the collective choice processes at the centre of the resource allocation process with a market, or decentralised, model that encourages the achievement of value for money. Flexibility in personnel management is an essential element of the latter part of the strategy, but made more difficult by the former.

NOTES AND REFERENCES

1. Handy, C. *"Gods of Management"*, London, Pan Books, 1985.
2. Peters, T. *"Thriving on Chaos"*, London, Macmillan, 1987.
3. Metcalfe, L. and Richards, S. *"Improving Public Management"*, London, Sage, 1987.
4. Stewart, R. "Managerial Behaviour: How Research Has Changed the Traditional Picture", in Michael J. Earl (ed.), *"Perspectives on Management"*, Oxford: Oxford University Press 5, 1983.
5. Cassels, J. *"The Review of Personnel Work in Government Departments"*, London, HMSO, 1983.
6. *Ibid.*
7. Fish, M. "The Post Office: Strategy of a programme for Change", in *Public Money and Management*, Vol. 8, No.3, 1988.
8. Efficiency Unit *"Improving Management in Government; the Next Steps*, London, HMSO, 1988.
9. *Ibid.*
10. Stewart, J. and Stewart, R. "Management in the Public Domain", in *Public Money and Management*, Vol. 8, Nos.1/2, 1988.
11. Peters, Thomas, J. and Waterman, R. H. *"In Search of Excellence"*, New York: Harper and Row, 1982.

PROMOTING FLEXIBILITY THROUGH PAY POLICY — EXPERIENCE FROM THE SWEDISH NATIONAL ADMINISTRATION

Lennart Gustafsson*

For some considerable time now, the public sector and its efficiency have been a focus of political debate in Sweden. Both Social Democratic and non–socialist governments have introduced programmes for reform and development. On certain points there have been differences of emphasis (e.g. as regards the scope of public activities), but in all cases the aim has been to make the administration more efficient, less bureaucratic, more service–minded and better attuned to the individual needs and preferences of the general public.

The present Social Democratic government embarked in 1982 on a wide–ranging process of reform aimed at modernising — "renewing" — the national administration, so as to achieve greater freedom of choice for the general public, greater efficiency, better services and a greater amount of democracy (in the sense of greater public influence, above all on local government activities).

In 1985 the government presented to the Riksdag (parliament) a comprehensive programme for the renewal of the public sector which included an important section on the development of the role of the State as employer since they realised that national government personnel policy was a strategic parameter for achieving the aims of the programme. Later the same year, the government followed up the renewal legislation with a Bill on future personnel policy. This Bill, which was passed by Parliament, represented a departure from the traditions which until then had guided the activities of the State qua employer. The Bill lays down that personnel policy is to be made an instrument for the renewal of the national administration.

Historical Background

Ten years ago, *pay policy* in the public sector was characterised by the following features:

- all rates of pay referred to posts, not individuals;
- the pay system was made up of salary grades, each post being specifically graded;

---

* Director, National Fund for Administrative Development and Training for Government Employees, Ministry of Public Administration, Sweden.

- the gradings of individual posts and rates of pay were decided centrally, often by the government;
- the structure of appointments was fixed by the government and lower levels by themselves had very little opportunity of introducing changes;
- the same pay system applied throughout the national government sector, including both utilities and defence;
- changes in the average pay level were usually based on adjustment to the movement of wages in the private sector;
- the scope for pay improvements was not based on the same principles as elsewhere in the labour market. The State was more strongly influenced by egalitarian ideals, with the result that the national government sector acquired a more horizontal pay structure than other sectors.

Other questions of personnel policy were treated in similar fashion. Uniformity was considered important and was achieved by means of a centrally adopted, detailed system of regulations. For example, it was at this very time that a new philosophy emerged in the Swedish labour market concerning powers of co–determination for employees. This philosophy also came to apply to the national government sector, which in fact concluded the first co–determination agreement, although it differed from agreements in other sectors by emphasising the limits of co–determination, i.e. specifying the questions on which national government employees, qua employees, would be allowed to exert influence and defining the procedures for doing so. The line of demarcation between co–determination and political democracy became a more vital issue than the purpose of the reform, which was to accommodate people's wishes for participation in the development of their own workplaces and hence to contribute towards greater job satisfaction.

Agreements in other sectors were aimed at harnessing the employees' involvement, their imagination and their interest in developing operational activities.

Things have since changed dramatically. True, much of the old state of affairs persists. But, as a result of the new focus given to personnel policy, the objectives of the State qua employer have been unequivocally defined as:

i) helping to balance the national economy;

ii) improving efficiency and making the administration more service–oriented;

iii) making co–determination both practical and concrete.

These objectives are to be achieved in two main ways: by adapting pay and personnel policies to the circumstances of different parts of the national government sector (*sectoral adjustment*); and secondly, by dissolving the central regulatory systems and transferring decision–making on personnel policy to lower levels while at the same time developing management methods by means of a more modern budgeting process (*delegation*).

Today, then, the State no longer has a single, uniform personnel policy. Developments can move in very different directions indeed, subject to specified budgetary and policy considerations. The State now frames its employment policy as a party in a market concerned to enhance efficiency and to secure its supply of personnel — and not, as previously, in the guise of a "patriarch" intent on realising certain egalitarian or other social ideals of justice.

28

Rationale for a More Flexible Personnel Policy

There are at least three reasons why a more flexible personnel policy can contribute towards greater efficiency.

  i) Personnel supply: a flexible policy will enable the State to recruit and retain the right staff. The State must be able to compete with other sectors, and this calls for greater responsiveness and better adjustment to market conditions of employment.

 ii) Motivation: if personnel policy includes rewards for achievement, this can enhance the interest of the individual in contributing towards activities. Unfortunately, there is usually little correlation between achievement and reward in public pay systems, since individual pay development is largely related to length of service and promotion is usually the sole motivating factor.

iii) Inertia in the system: two changes are needed here, one being the removal of inflexibility in the form of centrally decided organisational structures which tie appointments to fixed salary grades, the other concerned with reducing what is often a natural resistance on the part of the employee to changes, by clarifying the situation with regard to job security. Although tradition and expansion of government services meant that redundancies were very rare in the Swedish civil service, job security was, until recently, based mainly on political pronouncements rather than strict regulations. However, when reductions and major reorganisations were planned as part of the public service reform programme, a job security arrangement was negotiated with employees. This did not give any absolute right to a new post, but it defined the State's obligations to the individual in the event of cuts.

STRATEGIES FOR CHANGE

Sweden's national administration differs from its counterparts in many other countries as regards the division between policy and executive functions. The government departments (ministries) are small and their main task is to support the responsible Ministers in matters of policy (legislation, the national budget). Policy implementation is carried out by a large number of relatively autonomous national authorities, which between them account for the majority of national government employees. Civil servants are employed by the individual authority.

Nevertheless, conditions of service have traditionally been defined at *central level*, by the government or the National Agency for Government Employers, which is entrusted by the government with the task of conducting collective negotiations with the unions on conditions of service for national government employees. Recruitment and promotion, however, are decided "locally", i.e. by the individual authorities.

One of the most important reforms in the Swedish programme of renewal concerns the allocation of roles between the government and the national authorities. The budgeting system is now developing towards a more long–term approach, with national authorities being given three–year financial planning frames. Greater importance is being attached to the evaluation of results from previous periods, and these evaluations form the basis of a dialogue on objectives between the government and the individual authority. The intention is to introduce greater liberty for national authorities to decide their internal affairs, by allowing them to choose the means of achieving objectives and to control important aspects of organisation, personnel and pay policies.

The State, qua employer, has made use of four principal methods in order to achieve a more flexible personnel policy that is conducive to administrative development and efficiency:

— market adjustment
— decentralisation
— individualisation
— co–determination.

The system of personnel policy has been brought more closely into line with other sectors of the labour market. The State wishes to achieve harmonisation with the market by establishing conditions resembling those prevailing in the sectors with which the public employers have to compete for labour.

The employer's aim in negotiations during recent years has been for pay policy to be determined in relation to operational needs and labour supply. To make this possible, decisions concerning the allocation of pay improvements, and certain other aspects of personnel policy, have to be made by the persons directly responsible for operations. In a word, personnel policy decisions have to be *decentralised* from central level to lower levels, to the national authorities and administrative boards, and in some cases delegated further down the line within the national authorities.

Within the personnel policy system, moreover, the employer is trying to achieve flexibility by making the definition of rates of pay and other conditions of service more *individualised*.

Efficiency and job satisfaction are to be improved with the aid of practical, specific and non–bureaucratic procedures for participation and *co–determination* by employees.

THE EXAMPLE OF PAY POLICY

Pay policy is one of the most important instruments of personnel policy for streamlining the national administration, and it is also the field in which Sweden has made most headway. In its Personnel Policy Bill, the government defined the following objectives for State pay policy:

— wide pay differentials are to be avoided for employees with equivalent jobs in different sectors of the labour market;
— state positions in pay talks are to be more explicitly governed by operational needs and by concern to achieve an appropriate supply of personnel;
— the pay system is to encourage flexibility, decentralisation and delegation.

The efforts made by the State to pursue these intentions can be illustrated by referring to a number of reforms over the past decade.

Market Adjustment of Pay Systems

The Senior Executive Pay System

As stated earlier, rates of pay for national government employees have traditionally been defined with reference to the posts they hold. Formerly this applied to all national government appointments, but departures have gradually been made from this predefined system. A more flexible arrangement for top executives was one of the first steps to be taken in this direction, when the definition of their salaries was removed from the sphere of collective bargaining. A special board was set up in 1977 to fix their salaries. Initially, salary definition was based on a division of top executives into certain categories, the salary for each category being defined as a number of "supplementary units" over and above a base amount applying to all senior executives. In principle, therefore, the executive pay system still took the form of a salary grading system, albeit of a much simpler variety than the traditional structure. For example, it did not include any automatic pay increments on grounds of seniority, although there is a system of annual reviews.

The executive pay system was revised after a few years, and rates of pay are now fixed individually and in absolute figures, with reference to assessments of the individual executive's competence, which among other things is taken to include qualities of leadership, achievement and responsibility. Pay criteria also take account of the long-term need of the State to guarantee a supply of senior executive personnel. Market conditions, then, play an important part, as does the necessity of guaranteeing a certain amount of mobility on the part of senior civil servants.

Market Salary Supplements

Developments have moved in favour of a relaxation of the strict system of salary grading for other personnel categories as well. For example, "market salary supplements" were introduced in 1984 for key personnel whereby the parties to collective bargaining were able to award special supplements to individuals, over and above those conferred by the salary grading of their appointments. This arrangement was intended to facilitate the recruitment and retention of market-sensitive personnel.

Initially the system was handled at central level by the collective bargaining parties. Special supplements were set at SK 300 per month, but an individual was usually given three or more supplements. Later, a fixed number of supplements was delegated to individual national authorities to be distributed when the need arose. These supplements can be seen as a step in the process of making the pay system more flexible. They have to some extent been superseded by reforms of the pay system which have provided more flexibility for individual differences within the pay structure.

Absolute Figure Salaries

In recent years the possibility has been discussed of extending the application of individual, absolute figure salaries to other, non-executive categories, in order to break free of the inflexibility inherent in the traditional salary grading system.

The local government sector has been a pioneer in this respect. As from 1st July 1989, salary schemes and grades are being abolished for all salaried municipal employees. Rates of pay will then be determined in absolute figures for each individual employee. This development, which is probably unique by international standards, has materialised following an agreement with the employees' unions.

The local government agreement lays down the following principles for individualised rates of pay:

"Pay policy is one of several means of achieving operational objectives. Accordingly, pay policy must encourage operational improvements and must help to secure personnel supply in the short and long term."

...

"In determining the scope for a revision of rates of pay, consideration must be paid to the improvements of quality, productivity and efficiency which have been achieved in the activities concerned."

The reforms described here have been aimed at bringing national and local government pay systems more closely in line with conditions elsewhere in the labour market. These developments also incorporate elements of decentralisation where pay decisions are concerned.

Decentralisation of Wage Formation

About ten years ago, employers and employees set aside one per cent of the total wage bill to be distributed annually through the collective bargaining process at local level, i.e. by national authorities and local trade unions. The amounts to be distributed within each authority were carefully defined by central agreements. In the first year the local funds comprised only 7 per cent of total pay increases for that year.

The criteria for the distribution of local funds were stated in general terms and took into account the interests of both employer and unions. As a result, compromises in negotiations often resulted in the distribution of the available funds for pay improvements being decided with reference to seniority. Nevertheless, because the improvements negotiated related to individuals and not to the posts which they held, the new system was a departure from the strict salary–grade approach.

Local Funds for Key Personnel

Recent years have brought an increase in the proportion of the total amount available for pay increases that is distributed through local collective bargaining processes. In 1986, rates of pay rose by 8.8 per cent, 3.2 percentage units of which were awarded locally; in other words, over one–third of the total increase was distributed at local level. In 1988, almost half of all pay improvements (3 percentage points out of a total of 6.6) were distributed at local level.

The local funds of the early years were proportional to the wage bill of the authority concerned. This is no longer the case. Instead the size of the local fund is now contingent on the need of the individual authority to recruit and retain key categories of staff. This has resulted, for example, in utilities with a large proportion of highly trained technical personnel obtaining, in relative terms, larger funds than other agencies.

What is no less interesting is that the criteria governing the distribution of the local funds in recent years have put far more emphasis on operational interests than used to be the case. The funds allotted at local level must go to the categories of staff which are particularly vital to operations. This being so, the prospects of recruiting and retaining well–trained personnel are an important criterion.

This revised pay policy has already yielded encouraging results. The traditional imbalance between the State and private employers — owing to the State paying relatively more for unskilled jobs and less for those with higher qualifications — has been reduced, and recruitment problems have been alleviated. The decentralisation of pay determination has enabled the qualifications and achievements of individual employees to be taken into account for pay purposes, resulting in a shift of emphasis in fixing salaries from posts to individual employees.

Individualisation of Rates of Pay

One of the main principles of the new State personnel policy has been to make conditions of service more individualised. Several aspects of this theme have already been mentioned: rates of pay for senior executives are fixed individually in absolute figures and it is the government's intention to introduce absolute–figure rates for broader categories. A start will probably be made with other highly qualified groups whose union organisations have responded positively to the proposed change.

Incentive Pay

Another aim of the government's new pay policy has been to encourage greater productivity. In collective bargaining, the two sides have agreed to experiment with new pay systems in which a proportion of pay is linked to quantified productivity improvements. Great importance has been attached to involving the employees concerned in the design of the new pay systems, partly by allowing them to influence the structures and working procedures through which achievement is to be measured. Rates of incentive pay are usually based on the achievements of a group rather than of individuals, and great care is being taken to arrive at criteria which genuinely reflect improvements in results that are meaningful from the viewpoint of clients and the general public.

Up to now these experiments have been confined mainly to activities which have close counterparts in the commercial and industrial sectors. They have, for example, involved personnel employed on the care and maintenance of State–owned buildings, the staff of personnel restaurants and cleaning personnel. In the salaried sector, there is a group performance bonus system for employees of State law offices. This has led to an improvement in the financial returns of the law offices, while enabling the employees to acquire higher levels of pay.

Locally Generated Scope for Pay Improvements

Up to now, all local wage formation has concerned the distribution of funds allocated by the central negotiating parties. A new system adopted in 1988 enables the local parties themselves to augment the fund at their disposal. That is to say, if the authority itself, by means of efficiency measures, can realise extra savings over and above the rationalisation requirements defined by the government, these savings can be used by the local collective bargaining parties to make improvements in conditions of service. Since efficiency gains of this kind are frequently one–off matters, the official guidelines stipulate that personnel policy changes should not involve future commitments. This principle normally precludes pay increases. On the other hand, the national authority is free to choose other rewards, such as gratuities, study trips or free cars. As yet, however, only a few authorities have dared to exercise this new liberty.

Market Adjustment

Adjustment of Non–pay Conditions

It is part of the heritage of the State as a "patriarchal" employer that certain social benefits for Swedish State employees are better than those enjoyed by other groups in the labour market. In certain respects, however, other sectors have caught up with or even overtaken the State in terms of benefits provided to employees. This applies at present to pension benefits. There are also long–standing differences in benefits and conditions such as holidays, sick pay and working hours. Conditions in these specific fields are now gradually being brought into line with those prevailing elsewhere in the labour market.

There is another change which ought to be mentioned. For many years, the criteria of "standing" (seniority) and "proficiency" have been rated as equal for purposes of recruitment and promotion. As a result of the reform of personnel policy, critical importance has been attached to proficiency. It is only in cases where two candidates are judged equally proficient that seniority can decide the issue. This has augmented the prospects of recruiting personnel from other sectors, and it encourages competition for senior appointments.

Management Development Policy

The need to ensure a sufficient supply of competent managers and to develop management capabilities has come to occupy a central position in the government's renewal programme. This is a natural result of new demands being made on the national administration, and of the introduction of new steering and budgeting procedures whereby many decisions concerning the means of achieving politically defined objectives are entrusted to the heads of national authorities. It is part of the new management development policy to widen the recruitment base, by looking more systematically for candidates outside the national authority concerned and also outside the government sector. The flexible salary system has in this context made it possible, at least in some cases, to recruit very senior managers from the private sector.

A new function has been established in the Ministry of Public Administration to give support to ministries for recruitment of top managers. This function will both strengthen recruitment procedures and provide advice in individual cases (thus it contains an element of head hunting).

Directors–general have traditionally been appointed for renewable periods of six years. The new policy will make this more flexible in so far as the second appointment will normally be for three years. Transfers of directors have also become easier under the new system.

A scheme of continuous training for the most senior managers was started already ten years ago. Under this scheme all newly appointed heads of national authorities have to take part in a two–week seminar where Ministers and senior experts make contributions. Recurrent shorter meetings for senior staff are organised on an *ad hoc* basis a couple of times a year.

Security on Job Agreements

Jobs in the national government sector are by tradition extremely secure. Heavy cut–backs have been rare. However, the changing economic conditions in the late

1970s prompted a collective agreement, in 1984, on job security for national government employees. That agreement defined the measures to be taken by the State before an employee could be given notice on account of activities being scaled down or discontinued. Among other things the agreement includes a far–reaching undertaking to endeavour to find new employment within the national government sector for redundant employees.

The system is currently under review, the intention being to do away with the detailed system of regulations and substitute more flexible procedures. Financial and administrative support will be tailored to each individual adjustment situation. More importance will be attached to making financial resources available for the further development of employees, so as to prepare them for new duties, regardless of whether those duties are located within the national administration or elsewhere. The negotiations have yet to be concluded, but the parties are clearly inspired by similar job security arrangements in the private sector labour market.

Sectoral Agreements

As has already been made clear, the traditional State employment regulatory system covered the whole of the national government sector, including the State–owned utilities, such as the post office, the Swedish State Railways and the State Power Board, as well as the defence establishment and the civil administration. It is in the nature of things that activities in the various sectors make different demands on the substance of personnel policy. In some cases State activities are competitive, while in others the State has a monopoly. Steps are therefore being taken to divide up the previously monolithic structure of collective bargaining. Sectoral agreements now exist for four sectors — utilities, defence, the rest of the national administration and State–salaried teachers. In material terms, these sectoral agreements are still essentially similar, but as a result of future negotiations being conducted on a sectoral basis, their content will be gradually adapted to the different conditions applying within each sector.

Decentralisation

The new allocation of responsibilities between the government and its national authorities makes it possible for the latter to abolish existing inflexibilities in the form of centrally decided organisational plans or lists of appointments. The authorities themselves can now decide how they are to be organised and staffed. They are also at liberty, within the financial frame indicated by the government and Riksdag, to establish new appointments with salaries appropriate to operational needs and market conditions. It has already been observed that questions of recruitment and promotion are decided by the authorities themselves, the sole exception to this rule being the heads of authorities and their immediate assistants, who are appointed by the government.

Individualisation

During the 1960s and 1970s, when the public sector was rapidly expanding, the new skills and competences needed in connection with reforms and other changes could to a great extent be provided by means of new recruitment and personnel increases. All that has now changed. New commitments and the need for new skills can no longer be provided for by augmenting personnel resources. Meanwhile, specialisation is on the increase and there is a growing need for new professional skills in many fields. The renewal of the public sector and the development of services calls, in certain cases, for re–skilling. This has necessitated a systematic approach to personnel development. There has been a growth of interest in planning the development of individual employees, with reference to assessments of their interests and aptitudes in relation to future operational needs.

Many such schemes have been prompted by the computerisation of activities. The traditional role of the secretary, for example, has been transformed. Many authorities are therefore introducing systematic programmes of job diversification for this category: the boundaries between professional/technical officers and secretarial staff are being obliterated, and mobility between different traditional careers is being made easier. These developments, needless to say, are encouraged by the individualisation of rates of pay.

The most ambitious, co–ordinated programme of personnel development concerned senior civil servants, and was concluded in 1986. All heads of national authorities (Directors–general) completed a two–week course of managerial development, followed by seminars at the various authorities in which management groups discussed strategic future issues for their respective authorities.

A management development institute has been set up for the national government sector, offering both short–term, thematic courses and longer managerial development programmes.

Central personnel development programmes for the national government sector have been re–organised. These activities are now financed on a commercial basis, to ensure that they are brought into line with the true needs of the customers, i.e. the national authorities. The development of training programmes of more general interest is, however, still funded by the government.

There is a close connection between personnel development and personnel mobility, and efforts are therefore being made, in certain cases, to encourage mobility between different duties, both within and between national authorities and between the public and private sectors. To facilitate developments in this direction, the regulatory systems have been reviewed and provisions which stand in the way of desirable mobility have been eliminated. National authorities have, for example, been given greater discretion in defining benefits connected with geographical relocation (relocation grants, subsistence allowances and other forms of reimbursement).

Co–determination

New Forms of Joint Consultation

The knowledge, experience and attitudes of the personnel are a fundamental part of the process of change within the national administration. Effective co–determination for employees in the matter of working conditions is, therefore, an asset in the process of administrative renewal. The employee participation arrangements introduced during the 1970s have, however, incurred criticism on the grounds of being excessively formalised and bureaucratic. Critics say that they have failed to release imagination and commitment as intended.

For the further development of co–determination, the government has instructed the collective bargaining partners in the national government sector to begin experimenting with new, more specific forms of employee participation in planning and decision–making with regard to their own working conditions. The aim is to enhance the efficiency and service quality of activities and at the same time to improve job satisfaction.

In several of the experiments now in progress, experimental schemes of incentive pay are being combined with new procedures of direct employee participation in decisions relating to working conditions. These experiments are based on a conviction that, despite fundamental conflicts of interest on general pay issues, the employee and employer sides have a common interest in the development and streamlining of national government activities.

Parallel to the various efforts being made to develop bonus pay schemes and to add to the quality of co–determination, the National Agency for Government Employers — the central agency responsible to the government for personnel affairs in the national administration — and the main union organisations have jointly inaugurated seminars for the national authorities on the subject of productivity, efficiency and co-determination. These seminars, of three days' duration, are being conducted for a small group of national authorities at a time. The authorities are represented by their Directors–general and other key persons, together with representatives of the local union organisations. One basic idea is for both sides, jointly, to get down to the practical task of streamlining operations within the national authorities. One of the topics of discussion for the seminars is new forms of remuneration geared to productivity improvements. During these seminars the two sides are trying to define objectives for continued administrative development, as well as analysing actual problems and suggesting practical measures.

The National Fund for Administrative Development and Training for Government Employees

Some years ago the collective bargaining parties in the national government sector took a further step in their joint efforts to modernise the national administration. In the 1985 pay talks they set aside MSEK 300 (roughly US$ 50 million) for the financial and inspirational support of development projects aimed at realising the government's renewal programme and at contributing in the long term towards a strengthening of job security for national government employees.

The money is distributed by a joint employer–union committee and can be applied both to personnel development (through training) and to the development of new forms of organisation and management (mostly with assistance from external consultants). All of these projects are aimed at broadening the skills of employees and at intensifying their participation in development projects. Upwards of a hundred projects, spanning a wide variety of operations, are currently being financed.

The original plan was for these activities to be confined to a three–year period, but after only two years the collective bargaining parties decided to establish the arrangement on a permanent footing with additional funding.

CONCLUDING REMARKS

The transition to a more flexible personnel policy represents a major change in a country's administrative policy. It is not a self–evident, universally accepted reform

37

and can come as a challenge to established values and ideas of justice and impartiality. Implementation of the Swedish reform is far from complete. Still less have its merits or demerits been evaluated. But there are a number of "midstream" observations which may be of interest.

i) The employer, it is true, is the prime mover of the reform process, but the union organisations are important actors, without whose participation the reform can be frustrated. The Personnel Policy Bill was preceded by informal talks with the union organisations at central level. These discussions led to agreement in all essential respects except, of course, concerning national government pay policy. Decentralisation of decisions on pay policy requires agreements between the collective bargaining parties, dependent as it is on mutually accepted rules and collective agreements.

ii) Limits have been set to flexibility. It has been specifically declared that decentralisation must proceed with due regard for the potential advantages of an integrated central employer function. Basic agreements concerning changes in the general level of earnings and the quality of the absolutely central elements of conditions of service will, therefore, remain common to the whole of the national government sector. This will apply, for example, to sick pay or job security and also to the basic principles of co-determination.

iii) Decentralisation requires the parties at local level to develop their competence, and must not outstrip the readiness at local level to accept new tasks. The government has made this an express condition of the reform process. In order to develop the necessary competence, the State has provided further training for executives at different levels who are the local representatives of the employer.

iv) The attitudes of national government employees in general are also important. There are deeply rooted notions as to which matters ought to be uniformly regulated and on which matters local deviations are permissible. The introduction of new systems has had to be adapted to this reality, and this is one reason why most headway has been made in the pay sector.

v) Finally, it should be emphasised that the introduction of flexible personnel policies presupposes a general transformation of the government's control of the different sectors of the administration. The introduction of long-term management by political objectives, combined with more efficient evaluation (which, more often than not, is likely to include a budget reform), is essential in order for personnel affairs to be successfully decentralised. If this transformation is not achieved, personnel affairs cannot be adapted to operational activities, which of course is the whole point of flexibility.

CHANGES IN NORWEGIAN PUBLIC PERSONNEL POLICY

Per Laegreid*

In recent years, a growing number of OECD countries have developed comprehensive reform programmes for the public sector, entailing deliberate intervention by the central authorities in an effort to transform public administration into a tool for government policy. In Norway this trend is manifested in the government's modernisation programme entitled "The New State", which concentrates to a significant degree on questions of organisation and personnel policy within the public administration. The programme emphasises that personnel policy has a determining influence on efficiency and productivity: if public administration is to function well, the best possible use must be made of human resources. To accomplish this, a greater degree of decentralisation and flexibility in personnel policy is required. This paper therefore concentrates on two central aspects: delegation of personnel management functions and personnel mobility.

Standardisation and Decentralisation of the Personnel Management Function

The system of public personnel management in Norway is a mixture of centralised and decentralised elements. Wages and salary policy has traditionally been characterised by strong centralisation and co–ordination, and the pay system has been based on norms of solidarity and equal treatment for employees. In recent times, however, demands for greater differentiation in wages and salaries have gained ground. In other areas of personnel policy it is difficult to perceive the State as a *single* employer. Recruitment and other non–pay policies have been largely decentralised to individual ministries and agencies, resulting in a considerable degree of fragmentation.

In recent years there have been several political signals indicating a willingness to consider a more active public personnel policy in Norway.

Personnel policy has been put forward as a means towards efficient executive management, which suggests that it is entering a period marked by change and reorganisation and also implies that agencies should be given a greater influence over decisions as to which kind of personnel policy solutions should be adopted. Current reorganisation proposals reveal a trend towards greater local autonomy, entailing more

* Norwegian Research Centre in Organisation and Management and University of Bergen.

freedom from standardised systems and central authority. With decentralisation, control of the actions of individual institutions will not necessarily be less, but it will involve increased freedom of action in relation to central bodies. Such a reorganisation will pose new challenges for personnel management functions in individual agencies.

Personnel administration in the Norwegian public service functions within the state of tension that exists between central control and local autonomy, at the intersection between the right of the management to govern and the right of employee organisations to negotiate. The state of tension between central control and decentralisation in the field of personnel management will be illustrated by focusing on three personnel policy areas: the wage and salary system, co–determination policy, and recruitment policy. These three areas are characterised by arrangements which are general, but which provide room for local arrangements.

Wage and Salary Policy

Wage determination is regulated by a basic general agreement between the State as employer and representatives of the main unions. Central rules for procedure are stipulated by legislation. There are, however, forces drawing the system away from a national wage scale and the complete co–ordination of wage policy within the State sector. Norms of solidarity in wages policy and extra support to the lowest paying jobs are challenged by demands for greater differentiation in wage scales to take more account of market forces. The current trend is to provide some flexibility for decentralised negotiation, yet the State's need to retain budgetary control over wage developments limits possibilities for decentralisation. Delegation and decentralisation must also be evaluated in relation to whether, from a purely administrative point of view, the agencies are equipped to take on greater power. A centralised wages system has given the personnel management function in the individual agencies a relatively passive role, interpreting the rules and adjusting to decisions made at central level. With decentralisation, the role of local personnel management functions will become more important and there will be a need to develop the State's local employer functions.

Co–determination Policy

In 1976, the Norwegian government announced plans to establish general personnel policy guidelines which would cover the entire public service, so that a unified policy could be achieved, but this was not accepted by either the public administration apparatus or the unions. In 1980, an agreement for co–determination was entered into by the government and the civil service unions providing for formulation of large parts of personnel policy through local negotiations. The central agreement was a typical framework agreement which was to be supplemented by local special agreements.

The framework agreements for co–determination were made on condition that local special agreements would be entered into within a short time, but in practice they have taken much longer than planned and many local agencies have not concluded the agreements envisaged by the central authorities. This may also be connected with the fact that the different parts of personnel policy may be in conflict with each other. A standardized and co–ordinated wage policy gives little scope for shaping independent co–determination arrangements. There is little reason for putting a great deal of work into personnel planning if it cannot be followed up in wages policy.

Recruitment Policy ✓

Recruitment policy has mostly been the exclusive task of individual agencies. This large element of decentralisation is legitimised by the fact that it functions within clear norms for just and reasonable criteria and procedures, based on candidates' qualifications.

A number of general rules are laid down for appointment committees, specifying the rights of candidates, rules of practice and procedures. In consequence, recruitment policy may be seen as the sum of many separate decisions which follow clear rules of procedure, but where the actual criteria are not specified. From time to time, efforts have been made at political intervention to achieve a more standardised, unified and co—ordinated policy. But the institutions have been good at protecting their autonomy and, up to the present, attempts to reduce self—determination have had little success.

Decentralised recruitment arrangements differ from delegation in the fields of wages and co—determination in that line departments are more powerful and personnel departments are much more peripheral.

Different Expectations of the Personnel Management Function

As illustrated by the above examples, there are great differences between the State's role in determining wages and its other roles as employer. The fact that attempts at centralising and standardising personnel policy in the 1970s were not successful may be a result of the mixed system which characterises personnel management. The system has to live with the tensions between executive management and control, co—determination and decentralisation. Personnel policy is required to comply with values and ideals that can conflict: it is expected to ensure equal rights and job security, which encourages the State to function as a single employer; on the other hand, its goal is to promote efficiency, productivity and profitability in the individual agencies. This creates an unstable equilibrium where, over time, personnel policy alternates between giving priority to the different values.

Personnel units are having to undertake more and more complex tasks. They are rule users, yet they have increasing possibilities for choosing their own mode of operation. Centrally controlled arrangements demand a high degree of rule interpretation in local personnel units, while decentralised arrangements allow a greater degree of discretion. The government's modernisation programme includes plans for increased delegation of responsibility and tasks to local personnel management units. When the number of tasks increases, the range of roles is extended and the possibilities for role conflicts increase. Personnel staff are often faced with ambiguities in decision—making principles, role relationships, definitions and goals. These ambiguities may make it easier for the personnel unit to live with tensions and conflicts, but at the same time they may give rise to frustration and criticism among personnel officials.

The ambiguity with which personnel staff are faced may have its basis in the fact that the activities of the personnel management unit are loosely coupled to the primary goal of the institution. More weight may be placed on procedures and execution than on content. The question is whether the symbolic side of the personnel management function is important, while the substantive content of the activities is less central[1].

In the next section we shall see how changes occur in the pattern of mobility in the central administrative apparatus without necessarily being closely bound to conscious personnel policy control.

Recruitment and Mobility Policy

The Ministries in the 1970s: Life–long Careers in a Closed Labour Market

Studies of how the Norwegian central administrative system functioned in the mid–1970s showed that demographic processes had the characteristics of a classical Weberian bureaucracy. The principle of recruitment by merit was strong, and the careers of officials were largely controlled by the individual institutions in which they worked. This recruiting system had created an administrative executive which differed from the rest of the population in most respects[2]. For instance, there were profound differences in the representation of the sexes: only 15 per cent of the administrative staff were women. There was a life–long career system, typically within one ministry. Executive administrative positions could, as a rule, be gained only after long and loyal service. An internal and closed labour market existed, whereby ministries were well placed to reward and influence their employees. There was little exchange of personnel with the private sector: civil servants experienced greater career opportunities within the ministries than outside them, and the majority had no wish to leave when their probationary period was over. Those who did leave tended to move within the State sector.

A form of *institutional pluralism* existed whereby the civil service functioned as a loosely connected system of institutions, with employees primarily engaged in defending the institutions where they worked and the tasks allocated to them. Through life–long careers and gradual promotion within the hierarchy, they were exposed to socialisation and disciplinary mechanisms that had an integrating effect and promoted adaptation to the dominant cultural pattern of the institution.

The Ministries in the 1980s: Quota Demands and Market Pressure

Towards the middle of the 1980s, the traditional mobility pattern was exposed to attack from two quarters. First, demands for a more representative administrative apparatus led to attempts to increase the representation of women through quota measures. Ideas of representative bureaucracy and quota arrangements are not a strong tradition in Norway, but were given an impetus in connection with the growth of the equality debate and changes in the normative structure in this area during the 1970s. Towards the end of the 1970s, the government and the Storting (parliament) gave increasingly strong signals that the State administration should in principle mirror society, and attention was concentrated on discrimination between the sexes. Quota arrangements were made possible through legislation and an agreement regulation, and moderate sex quotas were introduced in the central administration.

Secondly, the closed mobility system was exposed to pressure from the market. From the end of the 1970s, the demand for special groups of professionals increased. The gap between wages in the State and the private sector widened, and it became more and more difficult for parts of the State administrative apparatus to recruit and keep qualified personnel. The closed internal labour market gradually became more open, and was legitimised through the government reform programmes for the public sector, where demands for deregulation, privatisation and market–orientated units contributed to breaking down the differences between the public and private sectors.

These trends are clearly exemplified in the Ministry for Petroleum and Energy, which was established in 1978. Studies by the University of Bergen show that it has a young and professionally differentiated staff compared with other ministries: the average age in 1985 was 36, and over half were under 33. Bachelors of Commerce have become as numerous as lawyers. The typical recruit is a young man who comes straight from an educational institution. The personnel profile of the ministry shows that attempts to achieve a more equal representation of the sexes through the use of the quota arrangement have had little success: only 22 per cent of those employed are women, very few of whom have been recruited through the quota system. Although the ministry has, since 1981, encouraged women to apply for vacant positions, and has an equal rights agreement which assumes a moderate quota system, the most important recruiting criteria are professional ability and seniority, and among six criteria given for ranking those appointed, sex is clearly the least important.

On the other hand, the ministry has developed strong characteristics typical of a market–oriented bureaucracy. The greatest differences from the traditional demographic processes in the administrative apparatus are found in resignations. A pattern of mobility has developed whereby many employees look upon their service in the ministry as a training period, which will increase their market value and make them more able to take a job outside the administration. Life–long careers have become the exception rather than the rule: one in four employees has less than two year's service, and only 34 per cent of the executives who worked in the ministry in 1978 were still employed there four years later. Both the extent and the direction of mobility differ from that in other areas of the central administration. To a large degree, the petroleum bureaucrats move to oil companies or other private industries. On the whole, possibilities for advancement are judged to be better outside the ministry than within it: in the course of one year 39 per cent of employees received an offer of a position outside. A consequence of this is that 42 per cent of those appointed in 1985 expressed the opinion that there was little probability that they would still be working in the ministry in two years' time. A pattern has developed which is already known from the USA, whereby employees in State control agencies go over to the firms they once had the task of controlling[3].

The possibilities for internal control through demographic processes have thus been weakened. The ministry has relatively few qualified applicants for vacant positions. At the same time, the short service time and good external career opportunities have undermined socialisation and disciplinary measures. The question therefore arises as to what type of considerations influence the behaviour of civil servants. Are their identifications coloured by their earlier loyalties, their place within the institution, or their future career prospects?

The general impression of the identification pattern of employees is that they are increasingly oriented towards private enterprise. The most widespread role identification is that of negotiator, and there are just as many who identify with the roles of manager or contractor as with the traditional role of judge. The rapid turnover of personnel makes it difficult to integrate employees in a common ministerial culture, and problems arise regarding internal leadership and co–ordination, exacerbated by the fact that internal conflicts are relatively strong. At the same time, comparisons with the petroleum companies lead to staff frustration and dissatisfaction with the rewards available in the public sector.

Variations in the identification patterns of employees are linked to more than one set of explanatory factors. Account must be taken of where employees come from, their current position and their future career expectations. Two factors stand out: the position of employees in the ministry, especially the department where they are working, and their technical or professional background. While the demographic processes of the Ministry for Petroleum and Energy clearly differ from the traditional pattern in the central administration, it does not appear as if there will be an equivalent change in the other factors which influence variations in employees' identification. It is especially the Bachelors of Commerce who exhibit a swing in the direction of identification with private enterprise, while the lawyers are closer to the traditional norms of the ministry.

Career prospects appear to exert a less important influence on role identification than socialisation through educational institutions and position in the organisational structure. That the petroleum bureaucrats often go to the petroleum industry when they resign does not necessarily mean that their identification as ministerial employees is decided on the basis of such future career aspirations.

Although the mobility pattern has changed in the period from the 1970s to the 1980s, attempts at deliberate control through the introduction of quota rules appear to have had little success, doubtless because it takes time to change well–established institutional norms. On the other hand, changes in the labour market have had major consequences for the composition of the personnel employed in the Ministry for Petroleum and Energy. The ministry is adopting a market orientation from the private sector of the petroleum industry. This is apparent, for example, in the area of wage policy, where wages based on a certain grade are about to be supplemented with individual rates of pay and the administrative fixing of wages is supplemented by market adjustments. There are also indications suggesting that developments in the petroleum administration are acting as a catalyst for the spread of such tendencies to other parts of the administrative apparatus.

The government's latest modernisation programmes envisage a more deliberate intervention in the mobility pattern to achieve increased movement between administrative units and levels. But earlier experiences show that attempts at control are filtered through the organisation's right to negotiate, and are affected by established traditions and labour market conditions. Consequently the result is often negligible. It is especially important to consider the role of civil service unions in the development of a comprehensive administrative policy.

The Role of Civil Service Unions

In Norway, the possibility of the government conducting a deliberate and planned administrative policy is severely limited by the power of the civil service unions. Between 80 and 90 per cent of public servants are organised in three large umbrella unions with substantial resources. Traditionally, these umbrella organisations have played a central role in the standardised and centralised wage policy in Norway, whereas the local union branches have been more passive. Any increase in delegation and decentralisation in the personnel field will reduce the co–ordinating role which the umbrella organisations play, thereby undermining their position.

This strong position held by the civil service unions means that decentralisation of personnel policy entails not only a delegation of the administrative right of control to the local head of department, but also delegation to a local bargaining system where the administrative management must take its place as one party in the negotiations with local employee organisations. Changes in the personnel field will then be more a question of *realpolitik* marked by political struggles between opposing interests than one of problem solving and planned changes.

Conclusion

Some general conclusions regarding reforms of personnel policy can be drawn from the Norwegian experience. Reform programmes are more a collection of reform ideas than unified strategies for change. The goals often include better service, increased efficiency, better work places, and more democracy by increasing the influence of both elected leaders and citizens. There is seldom an explicit discussion of the trade—offs between such goals. Reform programmes emphasise the efficiency approach without formulating the operational goals which such an approach demands.

One interpretation of the relevant reform programmes is that they have a low probability of producing either strong positive or clear negative results. Decision—makers are more concerned with avoiding a fiasco than with achieving success[4]. The solutions chosen are often vague. Great importance is attached to responsible control, design, a plan and a deliberate choice. But at the same time, it has to be acknowledged that reorganisation and change in personnel policy are a question of power, where consideration must be given to interest constellations and limitations in hierarchical authority, to established norms and traditions, and to market pressures. There is also a considerable diffusion of ideas and reforms across national borders. Modernisation programmes with strong elements in common appear almost simultaneously in several countries. In Scandinavia great emphasis is placed on decentralisation, prototypes from the private sector and adaptation to the market. Not least is this the case in the Norwegian and Swedish reform experiments[5].

To understand the possibilities and limitations in the personnel policy area, it is necessary to go beyond the efficiency approach which focuses on finding the best method of organising the public sector. Ambiguity, uncertainty and conflicts are more usual than clear goals, clear understanding of the means to the goal, and perfect control. It is necessary to analyse the complicated interplay between the partly conflicting principles of governance in the administrative system.

The conception of a majority governance where responsible political leaders can govern through directives and commands must be supplemented by a perspective which takes into consideration the fact that employees in the administration exercise considerable independent judgement. The hierarchical principle coexists with several other principles, including constitutional and ethical rules, principles of professional autonomy, the principle of the sovereign consumer, and the principle that affected interests shall be represented in the decision—making process, and that employees shall be able to influence their own workplace. There should be less talk of choosing between different norms and values and more questions about displacements in the goals and standards which are used by the administration. We are faced with a multi—functional system where the different principles are present all the time, but the proportions vary with time.

Changes in the personnel management function and the effects of these cannot be understood purely as a result of a deliberate personnel policy. Control based on political priorities is supplemented with the rights of the civil service unions to negotiate. At the same time there are strong traditions and norms, and when the demand for market adjustment increases, other control processes cannot be put aside. The State must live with contradictions and lack of adjustment within personnel policy when the proportions between different forms of control are disturbed. This is one result of the fact that several different and opposing functions must be taken care of at the same time.

A consequence of this is the need to implement an extended concept of effect[6]. When there are different considerations built into the personnel management function, the various actors will stress different consequences. In personnel policy this is expressed by some actors emphasising effects on productivity and turnover, whereas others are more concerned with their own interests, the level of conflict and the distribution of power. It is important to adopt a broad concept of effect, which besides purely economic impacts also includes the political processes that attempts at changes in personnel policy set in motion.

It is also important to be aware that comprehensive reforms can have a substantial effect on both performance and our image of performance. Organisational success is dependent on factors other than technical efficiency. It is often difficult to measure the real changes in performance, and changes are often evaluated on the basis of beliefs about appropriate organisational reforms. A possible result of personnel policy reforms is that they have greater consequences for how we talk about public administration than how it actually functions.

NOTES AND REFERENCES

1. Meyer, J.W. and Rowan, B., "Institutionalised Organisations: Formal Structure as Myth and Ceremony", *American Journal of Sociology*, 83 (1977) pp. 340–63.
2. Laegreid, P. and Olsen, J.P., "Top Civil Servants in Norway. Key Players on Different Teams", in Suleiman Ezra (ed.), *Bureaucrats and Policy Making*. New York: Holmes & Meier, 1984.
3. Mitnick, B.M., *The Political Economy of Regulation*, New York: Columbia University Press, 1980.
4. Anderson, P.A., "Decision Making by Objection and the Cuban Missile Crisis", *Administrative Science Quarterly*, 28 (1983), pp. 201–22.
5. Olsen, J.P., "The Modernisation of Public Administration in the Nordic Countries", Paper 1988/2, Norwegian Research Center in Organisation and Management, Bergen, 1988.
6. March, J.G. and Olsen, J.P., "The New Institutionalism: Organisational Factors in Political Life", *American Political Science Review*, 78 (1984), pp. 734–49.

MANAGEMENT DEVELOPMENT
IN THE DUTCH PUBLIC ADMINISTRATION
A REVIEW AND NEW TRENDS

L.J. Wijngaarden*

Structure of the Dutch System of Public Administration

Until the 1940s a central personnel department was part of the Ministry of Home Affairs and operated in a similar way to the civil service in the UK. In the years following the Second World War, central control of personnel management gradually diminished. At present, each ministry is responsible for its own personnel policy within the framework formulated by the Cabinet. The establishment and classification of senior (management) positions is still subject to the control of the Ministry of Home Affairs, which is responsible for co-ordinating policy on personnel matters and formulating policy proposals for decision in the Cabinet. In addition, salary negotiations for the public administration take place between the unions and the Home Office, representing the Cabinet.

Total staff numbers in the central public administration are 152 000 (full-time equivalent) in 13 departments or ministries. Middle management consists of approximately 20 000 persons, higher management of approximately 6 000 persons, and top management comprises approximately 150 persons.

Moves Towards Reform

A renewed interest in policies and projects for reforming the public administration in the Netherlands emerged in the 1980s. Elements in this process are: a reduction in public expenditure in general, budget cuts and staff reduction, reduction of the public sector in favour of the private sector (privatisation), administrative rationalisation and a rigorous decentralisation leading to a greater degree of control with respect to budgets, finance and personnel at operational levels.

This process was initiated by the work of a government committee that thoroughly investigated the efficiency and effectiveness of the Dutch central public administration. In the field of personnel management this committee put forward a number of

---

* Director of Personnel Management, Ministry of Home Affairs, Netherlands.

proposals to improve the quality of public management. Amongst others, programmes were started to decentralise personnel management to departments and within departments to operational levels in order to increase the flexibility of managers. In addition, a programme to increase the mobility of civil servants was set up under the supervision of an interdepartmental body, the Advisory Council on Mobility.

The introduction of the Mobility Programme was planned in three phases. First, departments were asked to draw up a list of positions that would be open for interdepartmental mobility. The second step would be to reach an agreement with civil servants in these positions on issues such as job rotation and terms of appointment. On the basis of this information the third step would be to set in operation an interdepartmental job rotation scheme supervised by the Advisory Council on Mobility. The total number of civil servants in the target positions was approximately 6 000. This programme was started in 1985.

The first phase, completed in early 1986, can be called a success. A total of 1 200 positions, approximately 80 per cent of the total number in the target group, were opened for interdepartmental mobility. The second phase, however, is still not completed. The implementation was and is hampered by a lack of commitment by top management and a lack of experience regarding management development issues such as staff appraisal and career planning. In addition, the Council that supervised this process had only an advisory role and no power to enforce implementation along the lines of the Cabinet decision. As a result, the Bureau for the Mobility of Civil Servants, a component of the Advisory Council on Mobility, operates merely as an executive search agency for the public administration. The Bureau is rather successful in this role.

Despite the weaknesses of the Mobility Programme, a beneficial side-effect has been that (top) management is now beginning to realise that a change from bureaucratic control to managerial control presupposes a systematic endeavour in the field of management development. This process is considerably strengthened and accelerated by recent hearings of Parliamentary Investigation Committees. Each came to the conclusion that one of the reasons for the failure of public policy projects and the incomplete implementation of government policies under investigation was a lack of efficiency and effectiveness on the part of the management, which appeared to be insufficiently prepared, trained and equipped to co-ordinate and control the projects. The most recent example was the introduction of a new and fraud-proof passport, where the Parliamentary Investigation Committee concluded that the management had failed on essential points.

New Developments

Although recent developments in the Dutch public administration in the area of management development are auspicious, it is clear from previous attempts that eventual success depends on a number of conditions: the commitment of political and top-management levels; a willingness at the highest political level, i.e. the Cabinet, to discuss matters related to management development on a regular basis; and finally, an agreement in the Cabinet on a global framework for management development in the public administration.

The Ministry of Home Affairs has prepared a proposal for the Cabinet along these lines. It includes statements regarding the percentage of vacancies that should be filled from the Management Development target groups, mobility and job rotation, appraisal systems and career planning, and the relation between Management Development and training programmes and facilities. The implementation of departmental Management Development programmes will be evaluated yearly at Cabinet level. To avoid the risk of introducing a rigid structure, implementation is decentralised and remains the responsibility of the individual Ministers. In addition, the centrally established framework will be set up in such a way that there is room for adjustment to the various specific requirements and cultures of ministries.

To support the departments in the implementation of management development programmes and stimulate new developments where possible, the Ministry of Home Affairs has set up a Centre for Management Development in the Public Administration, staffed by highly qualified experts in the field of management development. Departments can call upon the know–how of this service institution in the fields of selection and recruitment, appraisal systems, management assessment and self–assessment programmes, interim– and project management, job rotation and mobility programmes, and human resources information systems. The necessary funds will, at least in the starting phase, be furnished by the Ministry of Home Affairs.

Summary

At both (top) management and political levels, there is a growing realisation that the necessary reforms in the Dutch public administration can only be implemented successfully if accompanied by a systematic approach to and a serious effort in the field of management development or human resources development. Earlier attempts to introduce management development programmes failed because of a lack of necessary prerequisites: a systematic and integral approach was missing, with centrally established objectives and conditions, and there was insufficient commitment at political and top management levels. The change in policy that is proposed by the Ministry of Home Affairs can be seen as a logical result of past experience. The plans that are being developed use the same approach that has proved successful in many companies in the private sector. Management development programmes in the ministries will be based on a global framework established in the Cabinet. The progress will be evaluated, also at Cabinet level, on an annual basis.

MOBILITY AT SENIOR LEVELS
OF THE FEDERAL PUBLIC SERVICE OF CANADA*

The senior levels of the federal government of Canada — the executives and senior managers — constitute the Management Category, which represents about 2 per cent of the public service (4537 officials at the end of 1988, of whom 559 were women) with an annual salary bill of over $300 million[1]. The main objectives of its establishment in 1981 were :

- to increase managers' sense of identity and reinforce the concept of management;
- to provide greater flexibility to deputy ministers to deploy and develop their management teams while still permitting accountability;
- to provide a common and uniform conceptual approach to job evaluation and compensation for management;
- to implement more rigorous selection and promotion practices;
- to improve human resource planning and establish a training programme for managers.

Responsibility for personnel management in the Canadian public service has gradually moved from the Public Service Commission to the Treasury Board Secretariat, which now has charge of almost all facets of personnel management apart from appointments and promotion.

The Canadian public service still retains the concept of appointment of an individual to a specific position on merit and not to a level within the Management Category. The original proposals behind the creation of the Management Category would have permitted appointment to level, but it now appears unlikely that this will be implemented. It was felt that the introduction of appointment to level would underline to departments the idea of the Category as a corporate resource whose members were not "owned" by any particular fiefdom, while for the individual employee it would lead to presumptions of personal mobility, to lack of "ownership" of a specific position, and to a sense of corporate identity, as is exemplified in the Canadian military and the Canadian diplomatic corps, both of which have *de jure* or *de facto* appointment to level systems. The fact that the years since the Category was founded have coincided with years of slow or no growth, of attrition and of pay freezes certainly has not fostered this corporate identity.

---

* This chapter is based on a longer report prepared by the Planning Evaluation and Policy Development Division of the Personnel Policy Branch, Treasury Board Secretariat, Canada.

Managing the Senior Levels of the Public Service

Senior staffing levels for each department or agency are determined by the Treasury Board. Some flexibility is built into the system to accommodate fluctuating executive and managerial needs and availabilities. Departments are provided with flexibility of 10 per cent of the base complement positions (or a minimum of one position whichever is the smaller), to allow for special assignments involving senior officials. Secondly, where departments have employees who cannot be accommodated within the 10 per cent flexibility provided, Treasury Board may in special circumstances allocate a temporary increase for a specified period. Lastly, the Temporary Assignment Program was set up by Treasury Board to accommodate short-term needs (up to 2 years).

Vacancies within the Management Category may be filled in a variety of ways, including deployment within or between departments, competitive process, or other special programmes such as the Temporary Assignment Program (TAP) and Interchange Canada (see below). The option chosen depends on departmental career and succession plans, operational requirements, and the service-wide needs and objectives of the Category.

Intra-Departmental and Vertical Mobility

Although the Public Service Commission has the exclusive right to make appointments to or from within the public service, it delegates authority for Management Category positions to deputy heads in order to provide them with the flexibility needed to use and develop their management team effectively. The deputy head may move a manager to another position regardless of its classified level, provided the individual's personal classification does not change. Such moves may serve to meet operational requirements, to provide for employee development, to accommodate employees returning from leaves of absence or assignments, to revitalise those with performance problems, or to redistribute the workforce so as to avoid lay-offs or surplus manpower.

In its 1987 Annual Report, the Public Service Commission noted that, contrary to the situation in other occupational categories, there was little indication of plateauing or career blockage in the Management Category. The Commission went on to state that: "The average number of years in the same position has increased from 3.6 in 1983 to 4.1 in 1987 while the average number of years at the same group and level has changed by an even smaller amount. One explanation for the smaller change in the average length of time in positions in the Management Category relative to the rest of the Public Service is the early retirement programme of 1985, which had the effect of lowering the average age of Management Category employees. Nonetheless, the proximity of the average ages of Middle Managers (SM minus 1 and SM minus 2), Senior Managers (SM) and Executives (EX) suggests that in the future there could be problems of advancement to and within the Management Category. The respective average ages are 45, 48 and 49".

Progress in Removing Practices Restricting Mobility

In 1986 the Management Category was examined in detail by the Auditor-General of Canada. His report observed that staffing of Management Category positions is a "relatively closed departmental–driven process designed to respond to management needs" with no requirement to advertise or to inform members of the Management Category of vacancies. In 1986, according to the Public Service Commission, 27 per cent of all management promotions were not subject to a competitive process. The study also noted that those responding to a questionnaire conducted during the audit had expressed concern over lack of information on job opportunities and over application of the merit principle in promotion.

The subject of redeployment was subsequently examined by a Committee of Deputy Ministers which, in looking at statistics on filling managerial positions over the last few years, found a general consistency of movement. For example, in 1981, there was an average of eight redeployments and 13 promotions from within the public service per 100 Management Category employees; in 1986, the number of redeployments and promotions averaged 11 and 15 per cent, respectively. The Committee concluded that the frustrations being expressed by members regarding movement within the Management Category are not due so much to declining opportunities for redeployment or promotion as to the lack of information on when and how the positions are being staffed. It therefore recommended that information about opportunities for promotion and for redeployment across the public service be made readily available to managers. As a result, the Public Service Commission has decided to publish information on vacancies in the Management Category. Notice of current and anticipated vacancies is sent weekly to the head of personnel in each department and agency. The Commission states that this new approach will lead to a more open system and help members of the Management Category in meeting their career objectives.

"Interchange Canada" and the "Business/Government Executive Exchange Programme"

The Interchange Canada programme, operated by the Public Service Commission, has been the prime vehicle for effecting developmental interchanges for members of the management cadre with other levels of government within Canada. It has the goal of fostering understanding between the private and public sectors. Public servants at the senior level are temporarily assigned to the private sector, academic institutions, Crown corporations, non–profit organisations, voluntary associations and other levels of government; similarly, representatives of these sectors are assigned to the federal public service. Thus all participants gain experience in other work environments, enabling them to meet their own career objectives while helping to fulfil the corporate needs of both the host and sponsoring organisations.

There were 196 participants on Interchange Canada assignment as of 31 December 1987, an increase of 10 per cent over the previous year. Of these assignments, 51 per cent were from organisations outside the federal public service and 49 per cent were from the federal public service to organisations in other sectors of the Canadian economy.

In late 1985 a review of Interchange Canada concluded that, although more than 1 200 assignments had taken place under the programme since its inception in 1971, the important and specific goal of strengthening relations and understanding between government and business could be achieved more effectively through the addition of a programme specifically designed to bring about the exchange of federal government and business sector senior executives. Consequently, the Business/Government

Executive Exchange Program was launched in 1987 with the express purpose of improving business/government relations while fostering personal growth for senior executives with high potential by providing them with challenging opportunities. To support the Program, the Prime Minister appointed an Advisory Committee to oversee its development and operation. This Committee, reporting to the Prime Minister, is composed of chief executive officers of major corporations and deputy heads of selected economic ministries and also, as *ex officio* members, the Clerk of the Privy Council, the Secretary of the Treasury Board and the Chairman of the Public Service Commission. In its first eight months, eight executive exchange assignments took place.

Integrating Mobility Policies with Management Development

The important role played by training and development in maintaining a strong and well–rounded management cadre is recognised as one of the principal reasons for establishing the Management Category. The Auditor–General's 1986 study observed, *inter alia*, that a "perceived lack of attention by senior management to the careers of MC subordinates has led some to believe that no–one is looking after the interests of the Management Category". Amongst reform initiatives undertaken as a result of the audit was the creation of the Canadian Centre for Management Development. The Treasury Board, in announcing establishment of the Centre, noted that: "The government considers that a long–term commitment to enhancing the excellence of its management group is the key to efficient and effective management of public programmes. It has recognised that substantial improvement is needed in management training and development together with a new commitment to management research."

The current Management Category training and development policy gives direction in three areas:

i) Management Category members are required to take Management Orientation Training (from the new Centre as of late 1988) as they enter each new management level;

ii) managers are to receive additional training and continuing training as may be required, in particular in the areas of financial and human resource management;

iii) developmental training may be provided, through educational leave, executive development leave and interchange assignments.

The third element of training and development policy for Management Category members described above subsumes a variety of support programmes designed to provide for horizontal mobility. Theoretically, they serve both as a source of skills and as mechanisms for meaningful development assignments. Nevertheless, it has been noted that in practice those who take up such assignments often experience difficulty in reintegrating. It also appears that educational or executive development leave for any purpose other than scientific research is discouraged.

The Executive Development Leave (EDL) policy was approved by Treasury Board in 1971 and was considerably revised in 1984 to encourage job–related training which is directly linked to identified human resource and operational requirements. The present policy and the EDL Program it covers are designed to provide for certain unusual training activities that are not offered under other training policies. These might include conducting research at a university or institute; teaching at an educational institution; working with business organisations, provincial, municipal or foreign governments or with international organisations. The Treasury Board authorises such leave on a case–by–case basis and it is therefore expected that its use will be very limited. There is no employee entitlement to Executive Development Leave and it is not a sabbatical programme.

The EDL Program applies only to members of the Executive Group. Leave with pay may be approved for periods of up to one year and participants are provided with a written guarantee of employment on return. Departments must provide the person–year and the Executive Complement authority for participants.

Mobility at the international level is promoted by the Office of International Programs, which is part of the Public Service Commission and works in concert with the Department of External Affairs to increase the number of Canadians employed by international organisations. It also co–ordinates the temporary assignments of Canadian public servants to positions in governments of other countries and vice versa. During 1987, 13 Canadian civil servants took up such posts abroad and 11 persons from other countries were assigned to positions in the Canadian Public Service.

Equal Opportunities

In managing and administering the Management Category, the government tries to ensure that senior decision–makers are broadly representative of Canadian society as a whole — the primary concern being for women and francophones, although recently this concern has been extended to include visible minorities, the disabled and aboriginal peoples. Accordingly, the government has enhanced the mobility prospects of these under–represented population groups.

In 1985, the Treasury Board set a government–wide target that 12 per cent of the Management Category staff should be female by 1988. The target of 476 positions was exceeded (514), and new targets require 678 senior positions in the Management Category to be filled by women by 1991. Targets for 1991 have also been set by occupational category for the other three designated groups (disabled, aboriginal and visible minorities). It has so far proved very difficult to ascertain the effectiveness of integrating these other targeted groups into the Management Category. Out of obedience to the law and a profound respect for the privacy of individual citizens, the Canadian government relies entirely on self–identification by the employee or the applicant. Since many who rightly fall into these categories appear to make a conscious decision not to identify themselves, the validity of the statistics is doubtful.

Canada's official languages policy has implications for mobility, involving both efforts to ensure adequate representation of francophones in the Management Category and requirements that members of the Category improve their language skills if need be.

Outside Recruitment to the Cadre

Part of the key to staffing the Management Category is the concept of introducing "new blood". This can have a dual effect: first, as a means of bringing into the ranks of decision–makers persons with a broad background outside the public service; second, by bringing in talented people from target groups, as a means of ensuring that the perspective of those groups is represented in policy–making. Slightly over 15 per cent of all entrants to the Management Category per year are persons coming directly from outside the public service proper, recruited through the External Recruitment Office of the Public Service Commission. The leading sources of such recruitment are other levels of government, private industry and Crown corporations. Other significant sources are educational institutions, the Armed Forces and the Royal Canadian Mounted Police.

Other Developmental Leaves

Leave without pay (LWOP) for education and career development is another way whereby senior personnel may seek horizontal mobility. Officials on LWOP are not a charge against establishment regardless of whether the department pays them an allowance in lieu of salary. It is the policy of the Treasury Board as the employer that, on return from an authorised absence without pay, the status of the employee should be clear and unequivocal. Leave is permission to be absent from work. An employee who is granted leave without pay for any period remains an employee and, on termination of the approved absence, should be assigned to a position and put back to work. Despite the title, the granting of leave without pay does impose a cost on the government as the employer. In most instances, the leave forms part of a period of continuous employment with effects on severance pay, annual vacation entitlements on return to work and in some instances subsidy to continuing benefit plans. In cases where discretion may be exercised, leave without pay is, therefore, normally granted when there are seen to be benefits to the employer (for example, for employment with international organisations in the national interest).

In mid–1988 the Treasury Board President announced department–by–department implementation of the Self–funded Leave option following amendments to the income tax regulations to permit income–averaging for intermittent and extended periods of unpaid leave. "This enables employees to receive, for example, four–fifths of their normal salary for four years, with one fifth withheld in trust, and then take the fifth year off with the certainty of an income to sustain them, at the level of four–fifths of their normal salary".

Canadian Problems and Solutions to Geographical Mobility

In terms of the geographical mobility of its senior cadre, Canada shares problems common to countries where career moves involve geographical location over relatively short distances. The problems are exacerbated, however, by the sheer size of the country. By far the most serious of these is disruption of spouse's career, a problem to which Canada has found at least a partial solution. Where an employee relocates to another city, if the spouse is also a public servant (which in the case of Ottawa–based managers is quite frequent) that spouse may apply for a Leave for Family Related Purposes. This is an unpaid leave of up to five years, even extendable slightly under deserving circumstances, but perhaps more importantly it gives the affected employee a priority right to vacant public service positions for which he or she is qualified in the receiving city. This provision is not unique to the Management Category but is available to all civil servants. Special provisions have also been made to address problems arising from mobility between French and English language regions.

Separation from the Cadre

In terms of mobility out of the cadre, deputy heads have authority (which they may delegate) to approve and process all separations except release for incompetence or incapacity or dismissal for political partisanship. These are the prerogatives of the Public Service Commission. The Personnel Management Manual lists 13 grounds for separation of which resignation and retirement are the most frequent. Mandatory retirement at age 65 was repealed in 1986, so employment no longer automatically ceases then nor may termination be based on age alone. For the years 1984 to 1987 separations from the Management Category amounted to 5.7, 9.4, 9.3 and 4.6 per cent respectively. The increased attrition rates in 1985 and 1986 resulted from the implementation of government policies to minimise the effects of establishment reductions. A Voluntary Early Retirement Incentive Program was established for a limited period to encourage senior managers and executives to retire early, with a view to achieving staffing and salary reductions and improving promotion prospects for younger staff. A revised Management Separation Policy, established in 1986, is designed to facilitate termination of employment for senior management and executive personnel. Of 206 persons who left the Category in 1987, 111 were retirements and 67 resignations, and only 28 left for other causes such as death, revocation of appointment, rejection on probation, end of term employment, or release.

NOTES AND REFERENCES

1. The Management Category comprises six levels: executive levels 1 to 5 (EX–1 to EX–5) and senior manager level (SM). The highest level is EX–5. Above the Management Category are Deputy Ministers and senior Governor–in–Council appointments — officials who are heads of major departments and agencies — of whom there were 125 at the end of fiscal year 1987–1988.

ASPECTS OF PERSONNEL POLICY
IN THE JAPANESE PUBLIC SERVICE

Sachiko Ikari*

Introduction

The public sector in Japan, though expanding, remains far smaller than in other Member countries. The current total number of full–time employees in the central administration is about 1 180 000, made up of "Regular" and "Special Service" employees. There are 850 000 Regular Service employees of whom 510 000 are employed in ministries and agencies, and others are in departments such as the post office and forestry service. Special Service employees include Ministers, judges, Defence Service personnel, etc. There are about 3 230 000 employees in local government. Total public sector employment, in both central and local government, represents approximately 8 per cent of total civilian employment.

The employment system in the Japanese public sector is broadly similar to that in the private sector. Both are characterised by the following features: lifetime employment, no mid–career recruitment, frequent mobility, internal promotion, seniority, on–the–job training, uniform working conditions and no collective agreement system. These factors have an important impact on the flexibility of personnel management.

Recruitment

Staff are recruited directly from schools or university by means of competitive examinations and most remain in the same ministry, apart from a period of external mobility in the early stages of the career, until they reach the retirement age of 60. The fixed retirement age system has been in effect since 1985, and an early retirement scheme also exists. In 1986, about 36 000 employees were recruited to central government and about 41 000 left the service, a third of whom were aged between 55 and 59; about 7 000 reached retirement age. Because of the very high rate of staff retention, the future staff structure can be easily foreseen and any possible surplus of staff is controlled, not by firing, but by hiring fewer staff. Public and private sectors compete with each other only for new recruits, because of the system of lifetime employment, Lower salaries in the public sector are causing problems in hiring specialists.

---

* National Personnel Authority, Japan. This paper was prepared while Ms. Ikari was a Trainee with the Technical Co–operation Service, OECD.

Career Development

Each entering cohort or class is clearly stratified according to their performance in the examinations. The top, A level, grade is destined for senior posts, while B and C level staff are expected to become middle managers. Within a given class, seniority plays an important role in career development. Especially within the A level, selection, training and career development, including mobility and promotion, are together designed to produce a type of generalist administrator. On–the–job training, which is enhanced by frequent mobility within the ministry, is regarded as more important than formal courses. Broad understanding is also more important than specialised skills.

All the members of a given A level class initially advance at the same pace until they reach the rank of assistant head of division. Subsequently, promotion is determined by merit and personality factors. Those who are not able to get further promotion stay at the same grade, changing their departments. Owing to the pressure of younger staff waiting for promotion, an individual can hold the top post of "Administrative Vice Minister" for only a short period of time: generally two years at the most. When one member becomes Administrative Vice Minister, all his classmates and remaining members, if any, of classes which entered the ministry earlier must resign. The common practice is for an incoming top civil servant to find employment for his colleagues in either a governmental corporation or in a private sector firm.

Formal training courses for A level staff corresponding to grades in the hierarchy are provided on an interministerial basis. In some courses, there are participants from the private sector and abroad. These training courses consist of four stages: newly recruited staff, branch chief, assistant head of division and head of division. Attendance at these training courses is neither obligatory nor a prerequisite for promotion; all newly recruited staff participate in the training, but the participation rate decreases as people reach higher grades.

For B and C level staff, there is no established career development plan. Since 1980, however, a special training course has been instituted to prepare promising members of B and C levels for the post of assistant head of division, although only 50 staff can take this course each year. There is no system of sabbaticals.

Sectionalism

The staff's sense of belonging to their own ministry, which is sometimes criticised as "sectionalism", is strengthened by the lifetime employment system. Individual ministries often fight tenaciously for bureaucratic turf and attempt to define problems in ways which are favourable to the enlargement of their own responsibilities. In addition, the Japanese place great importance on consultation and achieving consensus. As a consequence, there is a tendency for departments to consult endlessly and, if consensus cannot be achieved, it is not easy to depart from the status quo.

Working Conditions and Labour Relations

Around 60 per cent of public servants are union members but collective agreements and the right to strike are forbidden. The basic principles governing pay and working conditions are set out in the Public Service Law. Like the Civil Law and the Commercial Law, changes to the Law are often considered undesirable and strong political support is necessary for revisions to be made.

The Public Service Law provides that working conditions for public servants should be determined according to general conditions in the private sector. The

National Personnel Authority (NPA), which is the central personnel agency for the public service, conducts an annual fact–finding survey in both the public and the private sectors. The comparison covers pay and other working conditions such as working hours and paid leave. The results and recommendations are submitted to the Diet (parliament) and the Cabinet but are not binding. The survey is conducted using a large sample of companies with more than 100 full–time workers, excluding agriculture, forestry and fishing. For pay, the results of the survey are used to produce a weighted average, which tends to be lower than the pay level of leading companies. As to other working conditions, the prevalence of particular practices influences whether or not they are recommended for adoption in the public sector. Consequently, new initiatives adopted in particular companies or industries cannot be introduced into the public sector immediately, nor can the public sector develop new initiatives on its own account since the Public Service Law stipulates that new measures can be introduced only if they already exist in the private sector. The pace of change in public personnel policy therefore tends to be slow.

Owing to these characteristics, flexibility in the public service is confined to frequent movement of highly qualified staff and the new regulations recently introduced for specialists, details of which will be discussed later. In other respects, the Japanese system is rather rigid.

Attitudes to Flexibility

There is little pressure from within the ranks of the public service for reform of the personnel management system. According to an opinion survey of newcomers to the service, the principal motivation for becoming a civil servant is to work for the public interest; working conditions and future career prospects are lower priority concerns.

"Quality circles", which play a vital role in the private sector, and which have attracted considerable attention from abroad, do not exist in the public sector.

Political support for a more flexible personnel policy in the public service is not strong. Most politicians give low priority to public service personnel matters as these do not appeal to voters. Moreover, the main clients of the government are industries rather than individuals, and they are interested only in policies, together with the government machinery and related procedures which directly affect them.

A public service modernisation programme known as "Administrative Reform" has been pursued since 1981, and the Commission on Administrative Reform issued a report in 1982 which has no binding force. Its suggestions for the public service personnel system included: overcoming the "sectionalism" of the ministries, strengthening interministerial training for managers, mid–career recruitment, improvement of conditions for specialists, promotion of merit system, introduction of staff participation in personnel management and flexible working hours. Some initiatives have been taken in the fields of expenditure control, manpower control, strengthening of governmental cohesiveness, deregulation and decentralisation. These measures respond to the high political priority of reducing the financial deficit and pressure from Japan's trading partners for a more open market. However, no significant changes have taken place in personnel management, except in the specialist area.

Because of demographic changes and improvements in the general level of education, the staff structure of the civil service is becoming top–heavy with older and highly educated people. This is leading to higher personnel costs and apathy of younger staff because of diminishing opportunities for promotion. There are also problems of mismatching between staff resources and emerging policy areas. The change from a manufacturing–oriented to a service–oriented industrial structure, the growing interdependence and multipolarity of the world economy and the increase in technological opportunities have important repercussions on policy priorities. Yet, under existing structures, staff cannot be redeployed easily or quickly in the public service. Problems of redeployment can be solved to some extent by training and increased mobility. Flexibility in recruitment and working conditions will also be required, although at present the traditions and culture of the public service are difficult to reconcile with such measures.

Responsibility for Personnel Management

The Central Personnel Agency and Individual Ministries

The NPA, the central personnel agency, is a highly independent organisation under the jurisdiction of the Cabinet and has an exceptional right to communicate directly with the Diet. The NPA is in charge of determining pay and working conditions, examinations for recruitment, retirement, firing, job safety, interministerial training, review of adverse actions and approval of employment in private sector enterprises after retirement.

Individual ministries are responsible mainly for selecting staff from among the successful candidates in the NPA's examination as well as for career development, including mobility, promotion and internal training. The NPA carries out random inspections of pay determination, working hours, leave and job safety in individual ministries. Individual ministries are also obliged to submit an annual report to the NPA on the number of staff recruited and retired, pay levels and internal training. The Prime Minister administers matters concerning manpower control, efficiency, welfare, and service discipline of personnel outside the jurisdiction of the NPA. The Personnel Bureau of the Management and Co–ordination Agency acts as a secretariat for the Prime Minister.

The NPA holds an annual senior level meeting with ministries and agencies to discuss current concerns in personnel management. In some cases, study groups are established in the NPA responding to the common interests of ministries and agencies in personnel management. The NPA also holds occasional meetings with representatives of the private sector and academics to discover their opinions about the public sector.

Personnel Division and Line Managers

Inside ministries or agencies, the personnel division exercises a strong influence. Staffing is determined by discussions between the head of the personnel division and the heads of divisions concerned. The post of head of the personnel division is regarded as one of the most important and prestigious, and to be appointed to this post is a stepping stone for a possible promotion to the top of the hierarchy. Line managers tend to pay less attention to personnel management, preferring to leave the responsibility to the personnel division. So far, there has been no attempt to delegate responsibility for personnel management to line managers.

Existing Flexibility in the Public Service

Although personnel management in the public service is relatively rigid, there are two important areas of flexibility: internal mobility and special measures for specialist staff.

The mobility of A level staff who have a university degree and are recruited to cadetships is relatively high. All of these staff change their posts once every two or three years, even though their grade remains the same. Mobility in the early stage of the career is considered as a kind of training for future managers, who are supposed to be generalists. Several years are spent in assignments to various departments within the ministry. The next step, although it is not applied to all staff, is to spend a couple of years overseas, possibly studying for a graduate degree, or perhaps serving as a trainee for an international organisation. After that, a staff member may be loaned to departments in other related ministries or agencies. Or, if a ministry has regional offices, he/she may spend some time in a senior position there. Generally, by his/her early thirties, the A level staff member has acquired a good deal of experience both inside and outside the government and is ready to begin the competition for the higher posts in his/her own ministry.

Interministerial mobility at middle or higher levels of the hierarchy is considered important for fostering cohesiveness of government, particularly as new administrative demands tend to cut across the boundaries of ministries. The basis of policy—making is "consensus of all concerned", and a close relationship with other ministries and agencies, which may be facilitated by staff exchanges, is useful. However, this kind of mobility of more senior staff is far less frequent than that of younger staff, although within the ministry, senior staff are subject to frequent rotation of posts.

Mobility is, nonetheless, neither obligatory nor a prerequisite for promotion, although staff with varied experience may have an advantage. Certain characteristics of the personnel system facilitate staff mobility. Individual ministries and agencies may re—assign their staff among posts which belong to the same grade. Most A level staff are graduates from prestigious universities, and they form a homogeneous body. Interministerial mobility can be arranged by bilateral negotiations between the ministries concerned.

B and C level staff, by contrast, tend to stay in the same bureau during most periods of their career and work as specialists rather than generalists.

Mobility between the Public and Private Sectors

Interchanges in this area are relatively rare, largely because of the special legal status of civil servants. Recently, however, it has become possible for researchers to hold a temporary job in the private sector and then return to a post in the public sector; this option is not open to administrators. During periods of economic growth, senior officials in the public sector often took up executive appointments in private companies after their retirement. This opportunity is now decreasing as the economy expands more slowly and companies tend to fill executive posts by internal promotion.

Employees in the private sector, especially economists, occasionally spend time in the public sector as trainees, although this is rare. During their stay, they are regarded as civil servants.

Flexible Arrangements for Specialists

Recruitment and retention of specialists who have a master's degree or a doctorate and are engaged in scientific or technological research in public laboratories is expected to become difficult. Salaries are rather lower than in the private sector, the nature of the research is generally less dynamic than that in private companies and funds for research are limited. Benefits from inventions made in the public service are shared by both researchers and ministries or agencies; researchers can obtain patents and ministries or agencies can use them without paying royalties. Promotion prospects for researchers are more limited than those for administrators because of the limited number of steps constituting their career ladder. Staff tend to stay longer in the same job, moving up the salary scale, and it takes a long time to reach a higher post involving greater responsibilities. It is not easy to transfer from a research career to an administrative one. This situation has prompted an increasing number of specialists to leave the public sector for foreign–capitalised companies.

In an effort to stem the outflow of specialists, a special regulation was introduced in November 1986. This initiative was taken in the context of giving high policy priority to the improvement of science and technology. The new regulation relaxes strict working conditions to permit flexible working hours and various types of study leave. Researchers now have the opportunity of working on a secondment basis for the laboratories of private companies. In addition, a few foreign researchers were recruited for the first time. However, no changes took place in pay and career prospects for any administrative posts, including senior managerial posts.

Conclusion

Changes outside the public service, such as the situation of the labour market, personnel management in the private sector, foreign pressure for a more open market and enhancing technological opportunities are important factors for the improvement of public personnel management. Frequent mobility, which so far has managed to respond efficiently to policy demands, is no longer enough and the need for greater flexibility in a number of areas is increasingly recognised. The new regulation for specialists represents a first breakthrough. The time may have come to consider the development of more flexible policies, although efforts should be made to seek methods compatible with tradition and culture.

MOBILITY IN THE SENIOR CIVIL SERVICE IN FRANCE

Jean—Pierre Ronteix*

All civil servants in France are bound by a special body of law and regulations, the *statut de la fonction publique*. It may seem paradoxical to look for mobility within a set of fixed rules and regulations, but the contradiction is merely superficial. Given the rigidity of the general framework, it has been necessary to incorporate a number of provisions to allow or even facilitate the mobility of officials, if for no other reason than to adjust to real life, which (even in government service) is a life of change.

What is worth noting in this context is that since 1983, mobility within both central government and local government levels, and between the two, has been a basic career entitlement for French civil servants.

There are many forms of mobility in the senior civil service:

— within the same department, whether within the same central government department, or else from a central government department to its external services, or *vice versa* (involving geographical mobility)[1];
— between one central government department and another;
— from the central government administration to the semi—public sector, ranging from public administrative bodies to "mixed economy companies" and including public industrial or commercial enterprises and state or nationalised undertakings;
— between central government and local government, which more often than not involves geographical mobility;
— between central government and the private sector;
— between central government and international or supranational organisations;
— between central government and the developing countries.

The senior civil service can be defined in various ways and the term "civil servant" can have widely differing meanings. For the uninitiated it broadly means anyone who is paid out of taxpayers' money. By contrast, in a number of official texts it means only civilian government employees working in a hierarchically organised structure. In this paper, we shall adopt a definition midway between these two and use the term to mean solely civilian (plus a few military) personnel performing an administrative function under the direct responsibility of central government[2]. In addition, the term "senior official" will be taken here to cover members of a "corps" of officials who have received their training either at the Ecole Nationale d'Administration or the Ecole Polytechnique and one of its institutes of further professional traini͏

---

* Maître des Requêtes (master of petitions), Council of State, France.

The scope of this paper is necessarily limited. It does not claim to be an exhaustive or detailed analysis of the formal difficulties, within the rules and regulations, that circumscribe particular kinds of mobility. The aim is, first, to explain as concisely as possible how mobility in all the forms just listed is possible under the existing rules and regulations; second, to consider a particular form of mobility, namely the two–way flow between the public and private sectors; and last, to try to assess how mobility is viewed by those primarily concerned, that is to say by public service managers and the senior officials themselves.

THE RULES AND REGULATIONS DEFINING MOBILITY

From the outset, the body of laws and regulations governing the French civil service has provided for a number of ways in which an official can serve in an administration other than his original one. These possibilities have been confirmed and even extended in the more recent versions of the rules and regulations. We shall consider first the different types of status, and then examine in greater detail a special case, the compulsory mobility of civil administrators (administrateurs civils).

Mobility for Established Officials

The standard practice is for serving officials to perform the duties attaching to one of the posts in their grade. If this were the only possibility open to officials, mobility would obviously be fairly limited except in the case of officials belonging to interministerial corps[4]. Fortunately, however, successive civil service regulations have provided for various types of mobility. By sanctioning the practice of making an official "available" (mise à disposition) while still on active status, the regulations currently in force have added a further useful element to earlier arrangements. An official seeking to move now has four possibilities.

   i) *Secondment* (détachement) allows officials, at their own request, to be seconded from their original corps while retaining the promotion and pension rights enjoyed in that corps; their salaries are paid by the corps to which they are seconded. Secondment may be for varying periods, usually from five to ten years.Secondment is very common in the case of senior officials wishing to serve in another central government department, a public body, a state or nationalised undertaking, an international organisation or in the overseas co-operation service; it is also the status accorded to officials who are elected to Parliament. In addition, the civil service regulations now allow secondment from central government to local government service and vice versa. At the end of the period of secondment, officials may apply to join the corps to which they have been seconded or to return to their original corps; in the latter case they are granted reinstatement as of right.

   ii) *Non–active status* (hors cadre) is the status assigned to officials seconded to posts not qualifying for a civil service pension, or to an international organisation, who wish to continue to serve there beyond their period of secondment.

In this case the officials no longer enjoy promotion and pension rights in their original corps, though they may subsequently be able to rejoin it.

iii) *Leave of absence* (disponibilité) has the effect of placing officials outside their original department or service. They cease to enjoy promotion and pension rights but may be reinstated in their original corps at the end of their leave of absence. Officials who move to the private sector have this status and must decide after a given period, usually three or six years, either to quit the civil service altogether or to return to their original corps. The conditions governing leave of absence vary, depending on whether or not the administrative authority accepts it as being in the general interest.

iv) *"Availability"* (mise à disposition), although in use for some 20 years, was given official recognition only in 1984. The officials remain members of their original corps, where they are treated as filling posts for which they continue to be paid the corresponding salaries, but they work in another department. "Availability" is decided on the basis of service requirements and the transfer may be to a central government department or a public body. This is a means of providing temporary assistance to a department or agency that is being set up or expanded and lacks sufficient high calibre officials. Officials can thus assist a new agency without forgoing the benefits, particularly financial, that they enjoy in the department to which they belong.

Measures Specific to the Senior Public Service

The four types of status described above are not restricted to the higher ranks of the civil service, but they are particularly suited to the special needs of senior officials seeking mobility. In addition to these general provisions there are a number of measures applying specifically to the higher ranks. They are of particular interest because they make it possible to move from the private to the public sector, including appointments at the discretion of the government, external nominations and non–established contract staff.

Appointments at the Discretion of the Government

The most important public appointments are decided by the government, which up to a certain limit (never apparently reached) can appoint people (public "figures" would perhaps be more accurate in this case) who are not civil servants. Appointment does not involve their being placed on the establishment of a corps within a department or service and, as in the case of civil servants appointed to these posts, the government has the same powers to dismiss as it does to appoint them.

In view of the fact that the posts in question are those of prefects, heads of government departments, interministerial and ministerial delegates, secretaries–general and ambassadors it is quite clearly possible to have mobility within the senior civil service if the powers that be are genuinely and consistently in favour of it[5].

External Nominations

For a given number of posts (usually three or four, but sometimes ten) filled by internal promotion of members of a particular corps, the government can appoint one person from outside the corps. In the case of external nominations involving the more senior grades, there is generally no additional requirement other than a minimum age and possession of full civic rights. In other words, the government can in this way, if it so desires, regularly bring people into the senior civil service not only from other corps but from the private sector as well. For example, among the senior members of the Council of State on normal service there are currently two former bankers, three former lawyers, two university lecturers and one surgeon who have been appointed through this system of external nominations.

External nominations have been traditional in most of the major civil service corps; in recent years it has been extended to ministers plenipotentiary (Foreign Affairs) and to the general inspectorates of various ministries (Act of 13th September 1984, as amended by the Act of 23rd December 1986).

Non-established Contract Staff

Here the trend is different, since governments have always sought, at least in principle, to curb the use of non–established staff, and some governments in recent years have even tried to bar the appointment of non–established staff to permanent posts within the central administration.

No measures have in fact been introduced requiring that such persons should be placed on the establishment, and a consensus does seem to be emerging in favour of maintaining the possibility of recruiting non–established staff. This obviously helps mobility insofar as it allows individuals who previously had been working in the private sector to be called in to assist in the management of a government department or agency.

It is generally accepted, for example, that computerising a ministry is a job for a computer expert hired from outside on a contract, even though the ministry may already have established officials who are computer experts. Similarly, when the Ministry for Cultural Affairs wants to recruit leading artists for particular purposes it can only do so on a contract basis, as the only way of meeting these artists' generally justifiable demands in terms of remuneration. Similar situations arise in the Ministry of Defence and the Ministry of Posts and Telecommunications, and more generally throughout the entire administration.

The approach used in one area could perhaps be repeated elsewhere, but this system is likely to prove expensive for the public exchequer and it is not easy to set limits on its operation. Moreover, in cases where contracts are renewed time and again the mobility aspect rapidly loses its significance.

Compulsory Mobility

Genuine mobility within the French senior civil service does not exist simply because the regulations contain some provision for it, or because the government can appoint whom it wishes to the most important posts, or because of the further possibility of external nominations and non–established contract appointments; there is also provision for compulsory mobility.

The establishment of the Ecole Nationale d'Administration (ENA) confirmed the resolve to ensure the mobility of senior officials. It could even be argued that those who founded ENA did so partly with the intention of putting an end to the segregation of the senior members of each ministry or corps which existed prior to the Second World War.

ENA was designed by its initial directors as a training ground for mobility: geographical mobility through the inclusion of about a year's training in a préfecture; sectoral mobility through the inclusion of several months' work experience training in business or industry, plus in some cases training abroad; and intellectual mobility through the variety of the subjects taught and the assignments arranged. It is thus no exaggeration to say that ENA is a form of training for mobility.

Clearly, however, this training was not enough in itself. The authorities, political and administrative alike, were soon considering compulsory mobility for serving officials. The creation of an interministerial corps of civil servants (administrateurs civils) to provide senior administrative staff for the central government ministries and agencies manifestly did not go far enough. It was felt, with some justification, that its interministerial character would remain purely hypothetical and that each minister or personnel director would confine himself to organising and using the civil servants assigned to his ministry on graduating from ENA.

This gave rise to the idea of compulsory mobility, initially set out in a decree of 26th November 1964 and currently governed by a decree dated 30th June 1972. Members of corps recruited via ENA, and Posts and Telecommunications administrators, are now obliged, after a minimum of four years' service in their original department, to undertake activities different from those normally assigned to members of the corps to which they belong or normally performed within the department to which they were originally appointed.

This compulsory mobility lasts for a minimum of two years and can be extended. The officials are assured of being able to return to their original departments, surplus to establishment if need be. This period of compulsory mobility is a prerequisite for promotion to the grade of assistant director (sous–directeur). It has therefore become an important element both in the career development of senior officials and in the personnel policy of each ministry. In a typical year (1986 in this case), 375 posts were offered in a so–called "priority list" published in the Official Gazette for young senior officials about to embark upon their period of compulsory mobility.

By virtue of its universal and compulsory character, its duration and the subsequent return of these officials to their original corps or ministry, this form of mobility has succeeded in establishing a genuine process of cross–fertilisation within the senior civil service. It does not, however, provide a complete solution since, in its present form, the system does not deal with mobility between the public and private sectors.

MOBILITY BETWEEN THE PUBLIC AND PRIVATE SECTORS

The Rules and Regulations

We have seen that the regulations allow transfers from one sector to the other.

The granting of leave of absence enables civil servants (and in this case they are mainly senior officials) to work generally for a period of between three and a maximum of six years in a private undertaking without severing their links with the civil service and, in particular, retaining the possibility of returning. They thus have a "fall–back position", something which is frequently held against them.

Secondment also enables officials to work in public bodies and even in State enterprises. Given the present size of the nationalised sector in France, the possibility of secondment clearly opens up a vast range of activities for the officials concerned. The public sector includes a competitive sector which is very akin to the private sector. State-owned Renault obviously differs from the Peugeot company, but the basic problems facing their management are much the same. In the field of banking and insurance, as a result of recent developments, the dividing line between the public and private sectors in France at present is so fine that it is easy to understand why secondment should be so eagerly sought after by civil servants who, while they may be serving in a public sector undertaking, are nonetheless working in a completely competitive area.

With regard to civil servants joining private undertakings, under Section 175-1 of the Penal Code, any civil servant responsible for the monitoring of a private enterprise or having signed a contract on behalf of the State with a private enterprise is barred, under penalty of imprisonment, from taking up a post within the space of five years in that enterprise or one to which it is financially linked. This provision, if it were strictly applied, would be a serious obstacle to movement from the public to the private sector. It would, for example, preclude government arms experts from being employed by firms working for the Ministry of Defence, government civil engineers from managing firms that undertake work for the Ministry of Supply, and Finance Ministry officials from occupying management posts in banking and insurance. But the provision seems very much a dead letter. It is felt that business ethics should be observed, but there are unlikely to be many cases where an official has actually been prevented from taking up an appointment of this kind.

There seems to be no equivalent legal obstacle to the appointment of a senior executive from the private sector to a post in the public sector. Nonetheless, it is a fact that there is far less movement in this direction.

When the government wishes to enlist the help of a particular individual from the private sector, it has, as we have seen, the means to do so through discretionary appointments, contracts and external nominations. If the people brought in from the private sector, where presumably they have been highly successful, do an equally good job in the public sector, they may stay in public service until age 65 depending, of course, on successive governments retaining them in their posts, which is not common given the political changes that naturally occur in a democracy. External nominations are permanent.

Under these arrangements France in recent years has seen a trade union leader become a prefect, several journalists and two businessmen become ambassadors, another businessman become director-general of a ministry and a number of lawyers and a surgeon become senior members of the Council of State. In addition, it is not uncommon for people from the private sector to be appointed to senior posts in ministries and government agencies.

In the case of contract staff, the situation is not entirely straightforward and successive governments have taken very different approaches. As the law stands, for senior appointments the government can propose renewable three-year contracts with no overall limit. Some government departments regularly use the contract system either for technical reasons, as in the case of the Defence and Telecommunications Ministries, or because of the special type of expertise required, as in the case of the Ministry of Culture, where some posts may call for artistic talents.

The regulations thus offer quite adequate scope for transfers, yet there is little movement from the private to the public sector, for a number of reasons.

Impediments to Mobility

Some difficulties lie in the regulations themselves (for example, the matter of pension rights in the case of those spending only a few years in public service). But three other factors are without doubt the major obstacles here: the different system of values, the way senior management is currently trained in France, and remuneration.

The Different System of Values

Although many senior civil servants are to some extent responsible for economic management in connection with welfare state policies and government intervention in the economy, their duties are mostly related to the sovereign powers of the State and hence often involve applying the rule of law rather than the rules of economic efficiency. This does not, of course, imply that senior officials administering the police force, justice, education, the armed forces and the diplomatic service ignore the criteria of efficiency, output, good management or cost effectiveness. On the other hand, it is equally obvious that the prime concern of managers in the private sector is the success of their business, even though they clearly have concern for the public interest as well as a sense of civic and social responsibility.

The difficulty cuts both ways: some senior civil servants do not perform well in the private sector, just as there are highly successful businessmen who have difficulty in adjusting to the rules and requirements of public service. Yet it seems more of an impediment to movement from the private to the public sector than in the reverse direction, probably because of the way senior executives in each sector are trained.

The Training of Senior Executives

The Ecole Polytechnique and, more recently, the Ecole Nationale d'Administration, were founded to train senior government officials. Through highly organised systems of switching between public and private sectors, their graduates have tended to secure the highest posts in industry, banking and, of course, political office. Though there are outstanding and noteworthy exceptions, the result has been to impress on young people, even those who are not particularly attracted by the idea of government service, that the surest path to the top posts in the private as well as the public sector is through the colleges designed primarily to train senior government officials. Consequently it is no surprise that many senior public servants switch to the private sector.

But no similar process is at work in the other direction. No student aiming at a senior post in the public sector would consider that the best way was via a management or business school, however prestigious, even though graduates from the Ecole des Hautes Etudes Commerciales regularly gain admission to ENA and often achieve outstanding results there.

Remuneration

There is no denying that earnings are higher in the private sector, as is both normal and reasonable. But it is equally the case that the desire for a high income is by no means the only motivation for the country's senior public servants. Nonetheless, it is always pleasant and satisfying to see one's income rise. To see it drop is always unpleasant, and sometimes unacceptable.

Enquiries undertaken by the writer would indicate that senior officials on leave of absence and working in the private sector might find their income halved when they

71

returned to their original corps. Those returning after a number of years on non-active status or after a lengthy period of secondment to take up a higher post in the service might also face a substantial reduction in earnings. Obviously the same process, but probably on an even more drastic scale, will operate in the case of a senior executive in the private sector who accepts a public service post.

This no doubt explains to some extent why no great pressure exists to appoint people from the private sector to those posts that are within the gift of the government. These posts are covered by the grade–related salary scales for the senior civil service and the salaries therefore are far lower than those for top positions in the private sector.

There is still the contract system. However, finance ministers have always been understandably reluctant to allow exceptional arrangements. When high flyers have to be attracted from the private sector, at extremely high salaries, their contracts require the intervention of the Prime Minister, or even the President.

In the case of the more average salary levels, the attitude of the financial services is somewhat more flexible. They are aware that the public sector needs some specialists from the private sector, but they have been able to take a number of precautionary measures to prevent excessive differences in salary, and they also fully realise that the lack of security implicit, in theory at least, in the contract system has to be paid for.

A number of senior government officials have given thought to ways of increasing the participation of senior business executives at the higher levels of the civil service. There have already been instances where senior executives from the private sector have been temporarily seconded to a ministry in order to help with the setting up of a particularly sophisticated operation. The debate on this subject is still continuing. Basically, it would seem that the best approach is an experimental one, whereby there could be some kind of agreement on the exchange of senior staff on the understanding that each side would continue to pay its former employees. Such arrangements would be more than a little unorthodox, particularly if these employees were to be entrusted with certain types of responsibility, but they should help to expand the exchanges between the private and public sectors and enhance mutual understanding.

MOBILITY AS PERCEIVED BY THE CIVIL SERVICE

Mobility has become so general in the senior French civil service that every official has something to say about it. Here we shall first consider the views of those in charge of the senior civil service, before going on to see how mobility is viewed by the officials themselves.

The Views of Public Service Managers

My enquiries naturally revealed diverse views held by the people currently or recently in charge of the senior civil service, yet there were a number of aspects on which they were agreed. For one thing, they were virtually unanimous in thinking that the public sector had gained from the fact that its senior officials had moved around during their career: this had led to a broadening of outlook, a cross–fertilisation of experience and ideas, an understanding of other people's problems, experience of other environments and relationships, an end to undue specialisation and an awareness of the need for departments to manage their human resources. Emphasis, in many cases, was placed on the benefits of geographical mobility.

Most of those I talked to would, however, like to see a more substantial return flow. In the case of movement from the public to the private sector, the original service, or the public service in general, can benefit from the experience acquired only if the person returns to the public sector. Most personnel managers consider, however, that this one–way movement is a risk that has to be run, and they are aware that returns would occur more readily if people who had left were offered career prospects which encouraged them to come back.

In any case, many feel that it is in the State's interest for management in the private sector to be aware of the interests of the nation as a whole and speak the same language as its leaders. This, of course, is greatly helped by the fact that many managers in the private sector are ex–senior public servants. Moreover, there are some, particularly among those in charge of highly structured and hierarchically organised corps, who maintain that this one–way mobility is essential to efficient management of their corps, bearing in mind that there are insufficient end–of–career posts. Some even take pains to ensure that those who "leave" are of a high calibre so that they enhance the prestige of the corps from which they come.

While emphasising that they were in favour of the mobility of senior officials, several of the people the writer talked to expressed concern about the "upheaval" among officials that may be caused, admittedly among other things, by this voluntary or compulsory mobility. It is not uncommon to see the entire management of a service change within the space of less than a year, thereby raising the problem of the service's "memory".

Some ministries are concerned about bogus compulsory mobility, simply a way of getting around the spirit if not the letter of the law, e.g. the appointment of an administrator to the general inspectorate of his own ministry. However, this seems to occur only very occasionally, mainly because the senior officials are themselves very much in favour of mobility, as we shall see.

The Views of the Senior Officials Themselves

While senior officials hold a range of opinions, they all seem broadly in favour of mobility. They are just as aware as the directors of personnel of the professional enrichment they derive not only from compulsory mobility but also from the type of voluntary mobility that they can arrange or accept when the occasion arises, as well as from geographical mobility when there is no obstacle in terms of housing or the husband's or wife's job. In some of the major civil service corps, functional mobility is a long–established tradition and a reason for the influence that these corps wield within the public sector and beyond, in society at large.

Mobility is also regarded, particularly by ENA graduates, as a means of switching to a different track within the public service, or outside it. If an official's ranking in the final examination at ENA means that he (or she) is not in a position to opt for the corps or ministry he (or she) wants, mobility and particularly compulsory mobility provides a good opportunity to enter this corps or at least to be assigned to the ministry concerned. If the early years in public service do not come up to the official's expectations, the different forms of mobility provide an opportunity of trying the nationalised sector or even the private sector, with the assurance of being able to return to public service should this experience prove even less satisfactory than the first. Lastly, it is clear that for all those who did not regard ENA or the Ecole Polytechnique as a ticket to a career in public service, but as a means of acquiring the most prestigious academic qualifications available, the continued existence of these various forms of mobility is a substantial attraction.

For all of these reasons it is understandable that senior officials, and particularly the younger ones, are very much in favour of retaining these options.

It is somewhat surprising that senior French officials are so little inclined to move outside their own country, despite the existence of a service for international civil servants which tries to attract people into this area. There can be no more than 200 or 300 top French officials working in international organisations. Financial and perhaps psychological considerations, rather than any legal obstacles, seem to be involved. In addition, reintegration is often rather unsatisfactory.

Notwithstanding these reservations — fairly minor in any case — it is true to say that mobility has become a widespread and welcome practice within the senior French civil service.

CONCLUSIONS

What, then, is the value of mobility in the French system? For the senior officials themselves, it is obvious: to be able to defer the final choice of career, broaden one's professional experience and put this to the test in a variety of situations, while retaining the possibility of returning to a post in government service. All these positive aspects are much appreciated by senior officials.

But is the benefit to the State, which employs these senior officials, quite so clear-cut? During the course of this analysis some drawbacks have been pointed out, e.g. an unduly rapid turnover of heads of department and the possibility for disturbing conflicts of interest, general and particular. These drawbacks could be substantially reduced, for example, if personnel management took more account of the interest of the service before authorising a particular move as well as through readier use, in the one or two particularly doubtful cases, of the regulatory and criminal law provisions barring an official from taking up employment with a firm with which he had in some way or another been dealing.

The disadvantages are nonetheless clearly far outweighed by the advantages that the French administration derives from the mobility of its senior officials: broadening of the mind, greater flexibility and a more comprehensive approach to problems seem the main benefits. They are substantial, sufficiently to allow the following comments without seeming to call into question the appropriateness of fairly general mobility.

First, the administration certainly needs experts of its own in some particular sectors. No one becomes an acknowledged expert in a given administrative or legal area in the space of one or two years, and no government authority, however lofty, can create an expert simply by appointment. The intellectual independence that is necessary to be recognised as an expert by all of the State's economic, political and social partners is not acquired through a mixing of functions. This comment may apply to only a few senior officials, but for them mobility does not have the same advantages; in some cases it may even have disadvantages. It ought therefore to be kept to a minimum for the groups from which these experts will be drawn.

Another, perhaps more contentious, issue is whether the State really needs "managers". We are thinking here of the State's sovereign functions, i.e. justice, police, the currency, defence. This is not the place for a detailed discussion, but it is debatable whether the criteria for the exercise of these sovereign powers are really the same as for management in the private sector, and whether the expertise and skills required are identical.

There is a major paradox here. The training received by senior French civil servants is held, both in France and abroad, to be of the highest standard. The vast majority of French firms try to recruit their senior managers and even their chief executives from the ranks of the senior civil service. At the same time, the country's political and administrative leaders are endeavouring to introduce private sector methods into government administration, even to the extent of bringing in managers who have made their mark in business. Given this situation, we might well ask whether it would not be more to the State's advantage to retain some of its more outstanding officials, if need be by according them special status and having them spend a lengthy period at a senior level in enterprises which are particularly efficient in the management of service activities.

Finally, one point to emerge from this survey of mobility within the senior French civil service is that senior officials, and personnel directors too, seem to pay insufficient attention to the international dimension. It is perhaps difficult to assess accurately what effects the Single European Act will have on the senior French civil service when it becomes fully operative after 1992. What is certain, however, is that French officials will find themselves competing in various ways with their counterparts from other Common Market countries. There can be no question that the more familiar they are with the methods and the people concerned, the better the French administration will be able to deal with the challenges it will have to face.

Thus, what the French administration surely needs more than the ability to speak the same language as the private sector is greater familiarity with the language and methods of its competitors. Mobility is a good means of achieving this, provided it is directed primarily to this end. To say that is not to belittle either the process of mobility or its value both to the State and to senior officials themselves. The sole purpose is to qualify to some extent the particularly favourable assessment that emerges from this analysis of mobility and its benefits in the senior French government service.

NOTES AND REFERENCES

1. The term "department" is used here to signify a ministry or other central administrative agency. A ministry may comprise several ministerial departments (e.g. the Ministry of Education, Youth and Sport) and may also have external field services which are responsible for implementing policy at the local level.

2. University teachers and members of the judiciary could have been included as well, but these two categories of government employee are clearly special cases requiring separate consideration.

3. The Civil service *corps* are groups of officials who have received the same training and/or are destined for similar types of functions. The officials belonging to a given corps are subject to the same statute and their career advancement takes place within their corps. There are both ministerial corps, which are specialised in particular fields (e.g. the corps of bridge and road engineers), and interministerial corps such as the civil administrators or the inspectors general of the administration.

4. Interministerial corps — see fn. 3.

5. The *prefect* is the government representative in a département (local administrative unit) or region, (regional prefect) responsible for the implementation and observance of laws and decrees, and for directing and co-ordinating the external services of the State administration.

   A *ministerial delegate* is a senior civil servant designated by a minister or a group of ministers (*interministerial delegate*) to represent the minister(s) in an executive capacity or as head of a service for the purpose of developing and implementing a particular policy.

MANAGING SURPLUS STAFF
IN THE SENIOR EXECUTIVE SERVICE
OF THE COMMONWEALTH OF AUSTRALIA

Rosemary Oxer*

Introduction

The Australian Public Service (APS) consists of 170 257 staff employed under the Public Service Act as at December 1987. The Senior Executive Service (SES) replaced the former Second Division and was part of the reform package set out in the Australian government's 1983 White Paper "Reforming the Australian Public Service", which was implemented in October 1984.

Within the Public Service Board, the then central personnel authority for the APS, a Senior Executive Staffing Unit (SESU), was established shortly before the creation of the SES. The SESU, through the Staff Development Branch, was responsible for staff development programmes for the SES and, through the Selection and Placement Branch in co–operation with Secretaries of departments, was responsible for promotions, appointments and transfer of SES officers. In recent times the Selection and Placement Branch of SESU has, in addition to the above duties, become responsible for SES Performance Appraisal, specifically within the Public Service Commission (formerly the Public Service Board) and more generally across the Service, and has acquired an expanded role in counselling, advising and negotiating with departments on staffing and personnel matters.

The SES is the top group of advisers and managers immediately below departmental Secretaries (Chief Executive Officers) who fill high–level advisory positions or control the Divisions, Branches and Bureaux which make up the Service. The SES structure comprises six levels, with gross salaries in 1988 ranging from $A52 720 (SES Level 1) to $A77 999 (SES Level 6). As at 30 June 1988, there were 1 500 SES officers, including 121 women. SES officers can be based anywhere in Australia or overseas but most are in the national capital, Canberra (76 per cent), followed by Melbourne (7 per cent) and Sydney (6 per cent).

Specific areas affecting senior executives in which the government made reforms were:

— more open competition for positions including from outside the Australian Public Service, with direct involvement of the Public Service Commission in the selection, development and placement of staff;

---

* Senior Executive Adviser and Assistant Commissioner, Public Service Commission, Australia.

- more emphasis on the development of managerial skills;
- greater mobility of senior managers in accordance with Service needs;
- more flexibility for departmental heads in the allocation and use of senior staff resources.

To ensure that Service–wide needs are taken into account in the staffing of the SES, the legislation divides responsibility for the management of the SES between the Public Service Commission and Secretaries of departments. Only the Public Service Commissioner has the power to appoint, promote and terminate appointments.

The 1983 White Paper stated that the SESU was established to:

- keep a central record of the qualifications, skills and experience of all SES staff and, on a voluntary basis, those in the immediate feeder levels;
- co–ordinate implementation of a suitable appraisal scheme for SES staff;
- participate, or be represented, in all staff selections to ensure that the highest standards are maintained;
- maintain a pool of staff who can be assigned to short–term tasks for staff development purposes or to meet urgent needs;
- advise on the redeployment or retirement of SES staff whose performance continues to be unsatisfactory; and
- develop programmes of staff development and mobility designed to promote equal employment opportunity at senior levels, to see that there is a sufficient supply of high calibre people to meet the needs of the Service as a whole, and to ensure that people are placed where they are most needed.

All except the last function are the responsibility of the Selection and Placement Branch of SESU, the other branch being Staff Development. The temporary assignment pool lapsed because the Public Service Board was not allocated salary and staff cover for the programme and good people with the specialist skills required were not nominated for the programme. The Selection and Placement Branch consists of less than 20 staff. The Assistant Commissioner (Branch Head) is also the Senior Executive Adviser and, while personally responsible for assisting all SES officers, has a particular responsibility for counselling and advising displaced (surplus) officers until they are placed or retire. For convenience in this paper "SESU" is used to refer only to the Selection and Placement Branch.

Prior to the Federal election of 1987 there were 28 main departments in the APS, with numerous other smaller bodies, associated with 27 Ministers. Between 1984 and 1987 a number of these departments held reviews of senior staffing structures and moved from structures based on positions at SES Levels 1, 3, 5 to ones based on positions at SES Levels 2, 4, 6. In making these changes one aim was to achieve significant overall savings in salary costs by having higher paid SES jobs but fewer of them. The results varied from agency to agency but the average saving was of the order of 10 per cent of positions and 7 per cent of total SES salaries. When these new structures were approved, the new positions were advertised (both within and outside the APS) and existing officers were required to compete for the new, more highly paid, positions. Not only did some SES officers fail to win positions because there were fewer total jobs, but in addition some people from outside the department, or even the Service, were promoted or appointed in preference to the "insiders". These displacements were sporadic and in relatively small numbers. As at 30 June 1987 there were 40 SES officers who were displaced under these circumstances and seeking substantive positions elsewhere in the Service. Six of these officers were still without permanent positions a year later.

Machinery of Government Changes 1987

Following the Federal election of July 1987, the Prime Minister announced a major reorganisation of the APS. The complexity of these Machinery of Government (MOG) changes will not be addressed here, beyond noting that the 28 departments were compressed into 16 under 17 Cabinet Ministers and 13 other portfolio Ministers, which created widespread confusion and anxiety in the Service generally. The amalgamation of departments resulted in job losses as economies of scale were brought to bear on non–programme areas (notably management services — personnel, finance, etc.). Other efficiency measures not primarily associated with the amalgamations were implemented and the government withdrew from some functions (for example, the naval dockyard in Melbourne was sold). In all, these changes resulted in estimated staff savings in a full year (after phased introduction) of some 3 000 positions including some 90 SES positions.

One of the main problems facing staff, individually and as managers of other staff, was the uncertainty surrounding the extent and timing of job losses. The Prime Minister had stated that there would be no compulsory redundancies and, while reassuring in one way, this left staff confused about what their status would be if their positions were abolished. It must be stressed that not all displaced officers (or even most) were inadequate or inefficient, but they were rather the victims of circumstance.

There were three other factors adding to the uncertainty. First, the Public Service Board (PSB) had been abolished and was being replaced by a much smaller Public Service Commission (PSC). The previous PSB functions of staff management were being devolved to departments and there was a hiatus period as the transfer was effected. (Comment will be made later on the role of the Senior Executive Staffing Unit which was transferred from the PSB to the PSC virtually untouched by the MOG changes.) Secondly, there were widespread changes of Ministers and Secretaries and it took some time for the top levels of management to settle down and address the administrative changes. Thirdly, the MOG changes occurred during the Budget sitting of Parliament, which is always a time of heightened political, media and policy activity and the administrative changes added a further layer of stress.

These far–reaching changes had an impact across all levels of Public Service employment. This paper focuses on how the problem of SES officers displaced by MOG and departmental reorganisations was handled.

Management of Surplus SES Officers

The government had already decided there would be no compulsory redundancies and, soon after the impact on the SES became clear, it reinforced this stand by deciding there would be no special SES termination payment to encourage surplus officers to leave. Whilst an Award of the Australian Conciliation and Arbitration Commission prescribes the redeployment and retirement provisions for non–SES officers, SES officers are "award–free" and rely on the Public Service Act for their entitlements. Section 76R of the Act did, and still does, give the Public Service Commissioner the discretion to offer an officer whose services he considers cannot reasonably be used in

79

the Service, a specified retirement benefit if the officer voluntarily retires from the Service within a specified period. He or she is then deemed for all purposes to have been compulsorily retired from the Service. This gives the retiring officers taxation advantages in respect of the retirement benefit and additional superannuation benefits. The Act also provides for the involuntary redeployment of SES officers to lower level positions, or their retirement under circumstances where the Public Service Commissioner is satisfied the services of the officer cannot reasonably be used in the Service.

In September 1987 the government endorsed the following procedures for the management of SES staff who were excess to requirements and made it clear that Section 76R retirements were not to be the first option:

— "In filling SES vacancies, Secretaries are required to give priority to the placement of suitable excess staff, including the possibility of offering placement at lower classification.
— The Public Service Commission is to satisfy itself that transfer action would not be in the interests of the efficient administration of the Service before accepting a recommendation from a Secretary for filling a position by promotion or appointment.
— The Public Service Commission is to pursue the placement of officers displaced as a consequence of the recent machinery of government changes in preference to offers of early retirement under Section 76R of the Public Service Act.
— A decision by the Public Service Commission to use its powers to offer voluntary redundancy is to be taken only after advice from the relevant Secretary and after consultation with the Committee of Officials overseeing the redeployment of excess officers.
— The cases of displaced SES officers already on hand at the time of the recent administrative changes are to be resolved as quickly as possible, preferably ahead of any machinery of government caused cases".

The Committee of Officials referred to above was established by the government to oversee the redeployment of SES officers displaced as a result of the MOG changes (a separate committee was responsible for the non–SES). It is chaired by the Deputy Secretary of the Department of the Prime Minister and Cabinet, and has representatives of the Department of Finance, the Department of Industrial Relations and the SESU.

Also in September the Public Service Commissioner stressed that:

— Women SES officers were likely to be affected disproportionately by the restructuring of Departments since most of them occupied Level 1 or Level 3 positions. Secretaries were asked to be aware of, and sensitive to, this situation so that ground gained through Equal Employment Opportunities was not lost.
— Secretaries had primary responsibility for trying to place SES officers.
— Secretaries were to keep staff in useful employment until they were placed.
— Secretaries could negotiate with other Secretaries to place officers temporarily or permanently. Staff could work in other departments and be paid by the home department.
— Secretaries could negotiate with the Department of Finance for cover in respect of officers eligible to retire within two years.

Displaced SES officers themselves were expected to make every effort to obtain a substantive position in the Service. They were guaranteed interviews for vacancies at their level unless they were assessed as clearly unsuitable on the basis of the application. On the other hand, displaced officers had only to be found capable of performing the particular duties of the vacant position to be successful.

Displaced officers were encouraged to consider the possibility of transfer to a position at a lower level if they were not placed within a reasonable period. An officer agreeing to transfer to a lower level position was entitled to remain on salary at the previous level for a period which was based on age and length of service. For officers of 45 years of age and over, or those with more than 20 years service, the period was 12 months while for other officers it was six months. Displaced officers, like other officers, could also retire on age grounds if they had attained the minimum retirement age of 55 years, or resign at any time, and in these instances they were not covered by Section 76R.

The Public Service Commission was prepared to offer a Section 76R benefit ("redundancy payment") to an SES officer where the officer:

— was not in a substantive job and was unable to be placed in his/her department within a reasonable period;
— had been unsuccessful in securing redeployment and, in the Public Service Commission's view, would not be able to be placed at their level within a reasonable period;
— was unwilling to accept redeployment to a lower level;
— was willing to retire with a Section 76R benefit; and
— where there was an economic benefit to the Commonwealth in retiring the officer.

Whilst voluntary retirement under Section 76R appeared to be a viable option, it was in fact used only as a last resort and, although voluntary, there was some sensitivity that use of Section 76R could be seen to breach the Prime Minister's undertaking of no compulsory redundancies.

The MOG changes of July 1987 provided a watershed for the APS at a range of levels and so, although not all SES displacements were related to MOG, that time is taken as a baseline to consider recent developments.

The Impact of the MOG

By January 1988, 153 SES officers had been displaced: of these, 40 had retired under Section 76R, 9 had retired on age grounds, 24 had been placed but 80 were still unplaced, 18 of whom had preceded the MOG changes.

As pressure was brought to bear to accept displaced officers, departmental Secretaries considered that their authority to manage their departments was being undermined. At times there was considerable animosity between the PSC and departments and, in addition, other officers saw their career options being limited by the "preferential" treatment given to displaced officers. To overcome this obstacle to the appointment or promotion of the preferred applicant, many selection panels found the displaced officers "unsuitable".

The concern that women SES officers would be disproportionately disadvantaged was correct: 12 per cent of women SES officers were displaced compared with 9 per cent of men SES officers. The women, however, were easier to relocate in other permanent positions. By June 1988, of fourteen women who had been displaced, seven (50 per cent) had been placed in permanent positions and one (7 per cent) had retired with a benefit. Of the remainder, four were considered difficult cases. By comparison, 125 men had been displaced, of whom 29 (23 per cent) were placed, 56 (45 per cent) retired with a benefit and nine (7 per cent) retired on other grounds. Several factors can explain this result. The women were, on the whole, younger than the men, had entered the SES more recently and were seen to be more in line with current management practices and style than the men. There is also the view, admittedly subjective, that women have had to be considerably better than men to have won jobs in the SES. At 30 June 1988, women accounted for 8 per cent of the SES, compared with 7 per cent in April 1987, 4.9 per cent in December 1985 and 3.9 per cent in December 1984.

Six months after the MOG changes several facts regarding the situation of displaced SES officers had become clear: organising temporary and permanent placements was an intensive workload for the SESU; displaced officers were becoming increasingly demoralised, there was growing evidence of physical, emotional and family stress and a number of officers were on medication and undergoing psychiatric and personal counselling; the Australian Government Senior Officers Association was becoming vocal in its concern for the way displaced officers were treated; and morale was low in the SES generally and this was extending to the feeder group of the SES. Increasingly, departmental Secretaries were finding it difficult to accommodate their displaced officers in terms of funding and work assignments.

The fact that most displaced officers were in Canberra (where 76 per cent of all SES jobs are located) was also a problem. Canberra, the national capital, has a population of only 220 000 and an insignificant manufacturing and industrial base. The large industrial and — hence employment — centres are Sydney (population 3.5 million) and Melbourne (population 2.6 million). Although a number of displaced Canberra SES officers would be attractive to the private sector, the cost differential in housing between Canberra and Sydney/Melbourne is so great that many officers could not afford to contemplate the change.

As departments, the Committee of Officials and the SESU informally reviewed the situation, it became obvious that, in addition to some remaining reorganisations flowing from the MOG changes, continuing displacements, admittedly on a smaller scale, would be a fact of life in the SES in the future.

The senior management of the Service was becoming increasingly concerned at the direct and indirect costs of having such a large number of displaced officers, and one large department engaged an outplacement counselling firm to assist in the handling of SES officers who were about to become displaced. Other outplacement counselling firms had also recognised the new market and approached departments and the SESU to promote their services. The Australian Government Senior Executive Association held a meeting targeted specifically at displaced SES officers and officers who believed they might become displaced, to plan strategies for changing procedures. At about the same time there were also personnel changes at senior levels at the PSC, enabling a further re-evaluation of the situation to be made by people who had the advantage of not having been involved in development or implementation of the previous policy.

By April 1988 two major developments had begun and continued concurrently through the next two months, resulting in a period of intense activity for the SESU.

The first offered greater personal assistance to displaced officers mainly via the establishment of independent assessment panels (chaired by the Deputy Public Service Commissioner, assisted by two other well respected senior administrators) and the provision of career transition counselling by a firm under contract to the PSC. The second was a short–term exercise designed to improve the quality of the SES entitled "Enlivening the Senior Executive Service". Departmental Secretaries were given the opportunity of having Section 76R voluntary retirement applied to SES officers who were *not* displaced and whom, in their opinion and with the agreement of the Public Service Commissioner, it was cost efficient to have retired from the Service.

These were significant initiatives and they will be described in some detail.

Independent Assessment Panel

The Independent Assessment Panel was set up to overcome the problem, faced by many displaced SES officers, of not having an objective assessment of their capabilities at their current substantive level. Many of the officers had been at that level for some years, had not had regular feedback from their supervisors, had difficulty in obtaining objective referee reports and, in addition, were being regarded by selection panels as less than equal to non–displaced officers. As already mentioned, this frequently resulted in displaced officers being found unsuitable for positions at their current level. The SESU suspected that in some cases this was not a fair assessment of the officers and was, in fact, a means of ensuring that the department concerned was not obliged to take a displaced officer but could take the applicant of its own choosing.

The repeated rejections by selection panels had a disastrous effect on many of the displaced officers and eventually rendered them unsuitable at their level, although earlier in the exercise this would definitely not have been a proper assessment.

The opportunity to appear before the Independent Assessment Panel is voluntary. The interview consists of two components: an assessment against the core SES selection criteria at the officer's level, and a discussion between the officer and the three panel members as to the officer's background, future aspirations and the realistic options which could be facing him or her. Referees are contacted and interview reports are signed by all members. The Chairman of the panel counsels the displaced officer, provides a copy of the report and discusses the panel's assessment of the officer. There has been widespread acknowledgement from the displaced officers that the exercise has been extremely useful, even though in some cases the officers have been told that they have serious defects against some of the core selection criteria or even, in a couple of cases, that they are unlikely to find a position at their current level. The reports are confidential to the officer and the SESU and are not made available to the home department or any other person. The officer may, if he or she chooses, use the report to support applications or to assist the career transition counsellor in advising on future action.

Career Transition Counselling

The career transition counselling has been provided by a firm of outplacement counsellors under contract to the PSC but with payment in respect of individual officers being made by the officer's home department. It has been clearly stated from the beginning that the counselling relates to the officer as a member of the Australian Public Service and is not outplacement in the sense of assistance in obtaining employment outside the Service. Acceptance of the counselling is voluntary but the SESU strongly recommends that officers accept the offer. The contract assumes an average of eight hours personal counselling per officer. Counselling covers three main components:

— personal adjustment to the reality of being a displaced officer;
— assistance with self–assessment;
— assistance with resumés, job applications and interview techniques.

This counselling has had a number of — possibly predictable — results. One is that displaced officers feel somebody does, after all, care about their general well-being. The counselling is concerned with the whole person and is not confined to the person simply as an SES officer. This is significant as the SESU is aware that some officers are undergoing considerable emotional and physical stress and that marriage and family breakdowns are occurring. As could be expected, more personal problems arise the longer an officer is displaced and, while not all officers have serious problems, quite a number have undergone medical treatment for stress–related illness. Many of the officers have volunteered that the counselling has been useful. There have also been clearly observable improvements in officers' general demeanour and outlook on work and there have been marked improvements in interview performance. This has not simply been at the level of presentation skills; officers have also demonstrated a better understanding of the selection criteria and their own strengths and weaknesses.

The Assistant Commissioner of SESU is not a trained counsellor and does not have the time for in–depth counselling but, even if this were not so, it would not be appropriate for the officer also responsible for overseeing promotions to interact at this personal level. For her part, the Assistant Commissioner has found it extremely valuable to have a professional counsellor to call on for advice. A close working relationship has developed whilst taking care to ensure that confidentiality in the counsellor-officer relationship is maintained.

Enlivening the SES

In April 1988 the government agreed that Section 76R voluntary retirement could be offered to SES officers who were not surplus but held substantive SES positions. This was possible because the use of Section 76R only for displaced officers was a matter of policy and not of legislation. The purpose of the scheme was to streamline senior management further by freeing up executive positions where, in the Secretary's opinion, the occupant was considered less than satisfactory (for reasons of age, health, personal problems, being out of step with the management climate or not meeting standards set by the Secretary). Nevertheless it was intended to be applied in cases where there were no grounds to take action on inefficiency. A deadline of 30 June was set for the exercise.

Departmental Secretaries were invited by the Commissioner to nominate SES officers for consideration for voluntary retirement and he examined each case to satisfy himself that it was a matter of poor performance and that the officer was not being subjected to unfair treatment. In cases where the Commissioner agreed, and he did in most, the Secretary or his nominee then personally spoke to the officer about his or her future.

Officers interested in taking the matter further were advised to meet with the Assistant Commissioner of SESU. During an informal private meeting the terms of voluntary retirement were outlined, stressing the fact that acceptance of the offer was voluntary. The officer was told what the dollar value of the termination package would be and a likely termination date was discussed. There was also discussion regarding the need to check superannuation entitlements and officers were advised to seek financial counselling if they did not already have a financial adviser. Officers were given a couple of weeks to consider the offer although a few made immediate decisions. Some officers were initially shocked at having the offer made to them, whilst others regarded it as an excellent opportunity to retire or commence a new career. Some officers were from departments which were undergoing departmental reorganisations, and this offered a quick and relatively painless way of avoiding the possibility of becoming displaced and going through the more lengthy process of being considered for other jobs or being asked to accept voluntary reduction.

From a total of 80 offers made, 60 officers accepted, one of whom was a woman. The average benefit per officer was $A50 610 and, in addition, officers received payment for accrued leave and furlough and had a series of options for superannuation, including a lump sum payment of the officer's contributions plus two and half times those contributions. The average age of the 60 officers was 54.5 years and the most common age (10 officers) was 57.

This exercise was considered highly successful by the senior management of departments. An important ingredient was the fact that each officer was given as much time as she or he required to talk the matter over in SESU and, until the time was running out with the deadline of 30 June, they were also given time to consider their final decision. Many officers commented on how quietly, quickly and cleanly the process flowed. One indication of the success of the venture is that a similar exercise is now being organised for the ranks immediately below the SES. The government has agreed to continuing limited use of Section 76R in this manner.

Lessons Learnt from the post–MOG Experiences

One of the main points which needs to be stressed, and which is frequently overlooked, is that not all displaced officers are inadequate performers. Some are technical experts but have less than adequate staff management skills, others are technical experts in fields from which the government has withdrawn, and some simply came in second in a strong field. It is true that some are, quite simply, inadequate performers.

One of the basic principles of the SES is that it consists of mobile managers. The problem of displaced technocrats becomes quite marked when they do not have broader management skills to assist them in being placed in other positions. This is a matter now receiving attention, and where outsiders are recommended for SES positions which require specialist or technical skills it is preferred that they are given term appointments rather than being taken into the career service. There is currently no provision for insiders to be appointed on term contract. However, some consideration is now being given in the PSC to creating a second parallel stream of the SES for technical experts who would, preferably, be on term contracts.

Many of the displaced officers were devastated by what happened to them. Many claimed to have no knowledge that they were regarded as poor achievers and had given little or no thought to alternative careers. There are, however, two sides to this coin: first, there has been inadequate counselling by supervisors and, secondly, there is a lack of self–knowledge on the part of officers. These problems will be addressed by the implementation of performance appraisal across the SES and a pilot programme is currently being implemented in the PSC; in addition, there is now a greater awareness of a need for career planning both by organisations and officers.

Many displaced officers would claim, with some justification, that there was little sensitivity shown to their personal needs. There are a number of reasons why this was the case, and the lesson has now been learnt and the use of career transition counselling, outplacement counselling and closer co–operation with, and use of, SESU is now apparent.

Individuals who joined the APS over 20 years ago believing they were embarking on a career for life proved especially vulnerable. They had given no thought to alternative career moves and were disillusioned and inadequately prepared for displacement. Many had a limited understanding of their long–term financial position.

One outcome of these experiences has been an increased awareness in SESU of the need to consider the officer as a person as well as the person as an officer. A series of SESU Occasional Papers has been started, the first entitled "Your Life and Money in a Changing World". The second paper deals with private sector models of human resource management which could be used in the public sector, the third is on performance appraisal and the fourth is on career planning. It is intended that these papers, which are provided to every SES officer, will assist officers in being healthier and happier in the Service. For some, however, it may help them reach the decision that they are not the right person for the SES and make the decision to try something else.

Conclusion

The two years after the MOG have been physically and emotionally exhausting for all concerned. Many officers have now embarked on different careers either as retirees or in the paid workforce. Officers in the Service have been made starkly aware that there is no automatic security in the APS and every officer should realise that he or she is potentially vulnerable to being displaced. Whilst being heavily committed in operational work, the SESU has also stood back and reviewed policies and procedures and put in place methods of operating that are designed to be efficient and effective for both the Service and the individual.

CONTAINING THE SIZE AND COST
OF THE IRISH PUBLIC SERVICE

James O'Farrell*

The Origins of the Problem

In Ireland, as in most OECD countries, the very definition of public service has proved problematic but there is now a consensus that it comprises all organisations which derive their income solely or mainly from the Exchequer. In practice this means the central civil service, local authorities, health authorities, security forces, education, and "non–commercial" state bodies. The definition no longer applies to "commercial" or "trading" state bodies, which are wholly or mainly financed from revenue that they themselves generate.

In 1970, the public service, as defined above, numbered 160 000 or 15 per cent of the Irish workforce. In 1986, it stood at 230 000 or 21 per cent of the workforce. The pay bill for these staff was approximately £2.7bn or 17 per cent of the Gross National Product. In retrospect, it is easy to see that there were two main reasons for this expansion: a basic inability, at central level, to withstand the staffing demands of expansionary departments and agencies; and a deliberate policy, introduced in 1977, to use post creation in the public service as a device to increase employment. The latter policy, known as the "Job Creation Programme", added over 30 000 posts to the public service over a period of three years.

It is not possible to account for the massive increases in the size and cost of the public service by reference to additional services or expansion of existing services. Admittedly, the demands on certain areas (e.g. social welfare) increased, and most departments and State agencies now have a European dimension, but other services (e.g. land reallocation, public building) have declined. More importantly, there has been massive public investment in new technology which *should* have resulted in a leaner, more cost–effective public service, rather than an inflation in staff of 45 per cent. In addition to the gross increase in numbers, the lack of critical analysis of staffing and structural proposals led to a proliferation of public service agencies and offices, many of which overlapped, competed against and duplicated each others' functions.

---

* Department of Finance, Ireland.

The Road Back

In 1981, the government accepted that the type of expansion outlined above could not be sustained by Ireland's relatively small economy. At that stage, measures to contain and reverse the trend were introduced in the central civil service. This sector represented only some 15 per cent of the public service but, as the only area under the *direct* control of the Department of Finance, it was the most amenable to restraint.

In July 1981, there were 33 000 serving civil servants, plus 1 500 vacancies which were in the process of being filled. These 1 500 vacancies were immediately suppressed (except for a small number where offers of employment had already been made). Then it was announced that, as vacancies arose in the residual establishment of 33 000, only every third vacancy in order of occurrence could be filled. Over the next three years, this rule (known as the "one–in–three" embargo) achieved a further reduction of 2 500. At the time, the embargo was criticised as arbitrary, inflexible, and anti–intellectual. But past experience had shown that policies which leave scope for arguments and special pleading are invariably undermined by so–called "special exceptions" that quickly become the rule. A blanket embargo, on the other hand, stifles such arguments and succeeds because of its very inflexibility and universality of application.

In 1984, a scheme was introduced which, unintentionally, undermined the effectiveness of the "one–in–three" embargo. In order to create some vacancies for school leavers, and also to benefit serving civil servants, the "career break" scheme was created, whereby staff could leave the service for up to three years (later five) and return after that period. The scheme provided that all vacancies arising thereunder could be filled regardless of order of occurrence. What happened, however, was that staff who would have resigned in the normal way, with no thought of returning, now opted for career breaks instead. They saw the scheme as an "insurance policy" in case their new careers did not work out, and were encouraged in this attitude by local management who wished to fill the vacancies if possible. Accordingly, almost the only vacancies now subject to the embargo were those arising from retirements on age grounds. As a result, and also because of some essential recruitment to the prisons service, overall civil service numbers remained static over the next three years.

In March 1987, the new government took urgent steps to reactivate the reductions both in the civil service and in the wider public service. In its budget statement of 1987, the government announced a complete embargo on recruitment to the civil and public service, except for a very small number of key posts which could be filled only with the consent of the Minister for Finance and the Minister for the policy area concerned. This policy, which also applies to career–break vacancies, continued through 1988 and is continuing through 1989.

Another measure used to accelerate staff reductions is a scheme of voluntary early retirement. This scheme offers an immediate pension and lump sum to all staff, regardless of age, in selected areas of the public and civil service where numbers surplus to requirements have been identified. For a while it was also available to all public service employees aged 50 and over. The scheme was introduced in late 1987 and ran through 1988. By the end of 1988, some 8 600 staff had left the public service on voluntary early retirement. In 1989, the scheme is on offer only to redundant staff, that is, those in areas which still have surplus staff. Basically these are specialist staff whose functions have been discontinued (e.g. land reallocation) or reduced (e.g.

arterial drainage), and staff of State bodies that have been rationalised, abolished or amalgamated in the drive to eliminate wasteful overlaps and duplication of activity.

As a result of the early retirement scheme and the recruitment embargo (which has been most firmly enforced), public service numbers were reduced by approximately 17 500 from March 1987 to the end of 1988 — a reduction of 7.5 per cent in less than two years. This included a further reduction of 2 500 in the central civil service, bringing the cumulative reductions for this area to 6 500 (19 per cent) since 1981.

Redeployment

In order to ensure that essential services are least affected by the recruitment embargo, a programme of redeployment of staff from areas of lesser to greater need has simultaneously been operated. Within the civil service, this has been implemented in three ways:

 i) transfer of general service staff to another department or office in the same grade: this has worked very effectively since 1987, mainly because staff may not refuse redeployment within their same grade;

 ii) redeployment of civil servants to different streams (e.g. converting draughtspersons to tax officers, agricultural scientists to inspectors of taxes): this cannot be enforced compulsorily and success has accordingly been limited. Out of an available "pool" of approximately 1 000 professional and technical staff in areas with surpluses, some 150 have accepted redeployment to other grades;

 iii) redeployment from one state agency to the civil service (or another state agency): this also relies on surplus staff voluntarily accepting alternative job offers, and the success rate has been very low — less than 100 redeployments out of a potential 4 000.

Outside the civil service, substantial redeployment has been achieved within the health and education sectors; for example, nurses have moved from closing hospitals to new ones and surplus teachers have transferred to vacancies in other schools. However, it appears that most public servants are not prepared to change career or organisation voluntarily, even from moribund or declining work areas.

The Future

Since March 1987, a reduction of 17 500 has been achieved in public service numbers, without any significant disruption in essential services. This represents a saving of some £200m per annum on payroll costs, albeit partially achieved at considerable initial expense arising from the payment of lump sums under the early retirement scheme (£100m approximately). These vital savings, so painstakingly and expensively achieved, could very rapidly be undermined if they are not consolidated and extended. For example, it would be economic madness to pay people to leave their jobs and then to fill the vacancies by promotion or recruitment. Yet the Department of Finance is under consistent pressure (from various sources) to do just that, and to fill all or most of the vacancies created by the early retirement scheme. In fact, there is as yet no room for complacency: the national debt amounts to 133 per cent of GNP and continues to rise, albeit at a much lower rate than heretofore. The public service still numbers 210 000, some 30 per cent higher than in 1970. The pay bill is approximately £2.95bn, which is still unsustainably high for a country with a GNP of £18bn and with such a high level of indebtedness. It appears, therefore, that strict discipline will have to be maintained over public service numbers and costs throughout 1989 at least. The scope exists for further reductions, without damaging essential services, and economic realities dictate that these must be achieved by the methods which have proved successful, with a firm embargo on recruitment and promotions, universally applied and supported at the highest levels.

FLEXIBILITY RECONSIDERED: SELECTED ISSUES

Colin Fudge*

The introduction of more flexible personnel management systems in the public service has largely arisen from efforts by governments to control and reduce public expenditure, to modernise administration and to seek increased efficiency. To be properly understood, these changes need to be located in their social context in terms of broader management ideas and wider economic and social processes of change.

Flexibility in its Social Context

As the 1980s draw to a close, notions of labour market flexibility and flexible personnel management have assumed a central role in strategies for overcoming economic recession and responding to increasing international competition and uncertainty[1]. Flexibility, argues Pollert, (1988), has been stressed as an essential component of economic progress[2]; it is a key element in current management thinking, and the need to increase flexibility has been put forward as a major reason for recasting labour legislation and developing new forms of employment outside the full–time, "permanent" contract[3]. Flexibility and flexible personnel management policies are seen as "new" and "modern" and are accorded considerable legitimacy. Some commentators, however, point out that many of the "new" practices are not dissimilar to earlier approaches that exploited a cheap and variable workforce[4].

In Britain the terms "core" and "periphery", and "functional" and "numerical" flexibility, developed from the model of the "flexible firm"[5], are now common discourse in industrial bargaining contexts and are raised as evidence of new management strategy[6]. The flexible firm, Pollert argues, connects two major strands of management thought in the 1980s: the Japanese model of production organisation and labour market structure, and notions of "strategic management" originating in the United States. It attempts to integrate these themes into a management strategy for appropriate restructuring at a time of recession. What is interesting in our context is how these broad private sector ideas are being diffused into the public sector and, in particular, their impact on reforms of central state bureaucracies. They clearly provide an influential social context, but are also more directly transferred through the high value and legitimacy they are accorded, particularly if they stem from "leading edge" companies.

* School for Advanced Urban Studies, University of Bristol, United Kingdom.

In carrying out major restructuring, the public service in a number of countries has taken on board certain of these private sector management methods, including the introduction of more flexible personnel practices. It is useful to recapitulate briefly the motives involved.

Expenditure Restraint

A key element in government expenditure restraint programmes has been the realisation of savings on staffing costs, mainly through staffing reductions. To facilitate the achievement of staff reduction targets, governments are introducing simpler procedures for redeploying surplus staff, terminating employment and enabling early retirement. It can also be argued that the introduction of flexible employment practices, such as part-time work, job sharing and short-term contract employment, appears to be prompted as much by cost-saving considerations as by other reasons. Expenditure restraint and staff reduction policies have tended to involve ministries and agencies being asked to determine how their own savings should be implemented. This approach fits with a demand from ministries and agencies for increased freedom from central control in areas such as organisational form and personnel management, reallocation of expenditure, and negotiations with unions and the workforce.

Ministries of Finance, however, whilst encouraging or directing expenditure restraint programmes and their "local" implementation, are generally opposed to any significant decentralisation to ministries and agencies, owing to fears of loss of control over expenditure. This reluctance to loosen controls is often mirrored within ministries and agencies, between personnel and finance sections and line managers.

Modernisation and Reform

In most OECD countries administrative modernisation programmes have accompanied expenditure restraint policies in an attempt to achieve a more efficient and effective administration. Administrative reform has involved not only structural change, but often also efforts to transform the traditional administrative culture. The initial emphasis has tended to be on financial management and efficiency, but there has followed increasing interest in changing personnel management systems by loosening central controls, decentralising personnel management functions to ministries and agencies, and delegating to line management.

Efforts to inculcate a new public management culture in the public service have led to a variety of changes in personnel management. Improved management training and career planning, more flexible career patterns, increased mobility, the introduction of open competition for posts, and promotion of a performance-oriented culture have all been variously employed. At the same time, concepts of service to the public, consumer orientation and democratisation of services are being pursued in some countries, and a number are coping with the additional challenges of competition, contracting out and privatisation.

Alongside these moves towards improved management, governments in a number of countries are seeking to increase political control over the administration. For example, appointments at the most senior levels have been brought more closely under the control of Ministers, and measures such as "high reward-high risk" contracts, with removal a potential outcome of unsatisfactory performance, have been put in place to increase the accountability of senior public servants for their performance and to make them more responsive to changing policy priorities.

Labour Market Competition

Reference has already been made to restructuring in the private sector, which forms an important context for public service change. These broader changes leading to restructuring are affecting the labour market as a whole. The public service, as it has expanded, has become less isolated from the external labour market and is increasingly in competition with the private sector in terms of pay, conditions of service and the working environment. As a result, public service personnel management systems are undergoing changes similar to, and in some cases based on, those in the private sector. Skill shortages, regional variations in labour supply and demographic changes are all leading to more flexible pay and grading structures and, in some cases, improved conditions of employment. In addition, the introduction of new information technology and the promotion of equal opportunity in the labour market are changing the shape of organisations and associated personnel management systems.

In summary, expenditure restraint, efforts to modernise the administration and changing labour market conditions together provide the impetus for change in public service personnel management.

The pressures for change and the resulting policy initiatives have been discussed in other papers in this collection. The purpose of the remainder of this paper is to reflect on a number of issues arising from the foregoing discussion.

The Public Sector–Private Sector Relationship

In the past five to ten years we have witnessed attempts to blur the distinction between the public and private sectors and a recognition of their interdependence in terms of national economic performance and productivity. Dissemination of private sector ideas, new management theories, ideological shifts towards the Right and business sector methods, and the threat and challenge of privatisation and competition policies have strengthened the notion that private sector ideas can be transferred for use in the public service. Through these changes the public sector will become, it is argued, a more efficient partner to the private sector in terms of national productivity. This argument does not enjoy universal acceptance and there are doubts about the utility of private sector methods in the public sector. Nevertheless, there is widespread interest in management ideas, in some private sector operational methods and, in particular, in the concept of "public management".

Perry and Kraemer introduced the term "public management", and the meaning they attach to it is "...a merger of the normative orientation of traditional public administration and the instrumental orientation of generic management"[7]. By the normative orientation of public administration they appear to mean a concern with issues of accountability and democracy and with values such as consistency, equity and equality, the assumption being that these issues and values are more salient in the public sector than in the business world.

Although some of the findings from studies of private sector management are clearly relevant to public service managers, we cannot overlook the differences that exist between the public and private sectors. The clearest of these differences are the political limitations on managerial activity, the permeability of organisational boundaries between public sector activities, and the absence of signals or measurable outputs comparable with the power of the profit indicator. Experience has shown that some private sector ideas and methods have not worked very successfully in the public sector, or have been frustrated by organisational, political and professional opposition and resistance.

One of the dangers in some of the arguments about efficiency and productivity incorporating notions of flexibility in terms of personnel policies is that their primary focus is on the *mechanisms* for accomplishing the objectives being set, rather than on policy and its derivation. A number of commentators have deplored the policy/implementation or policy/management distinction as a crude simplification that allows the value issues of politics to be put aside in favour of the more limited issue of how to perform more efficiently. Some OECD governments could perhaps reflect on this, since pursuit of efficiency and expenditure reduction may be carried out in a policy vacuum.

Commenting on their experience of working in both the public and private sectors, consultants such as Karl Weick, Warren Bennis and James March have noted how in the private sector the dominant assumption is characterised by its focus on *management as the rationalising force in organisations*. The public service, they argue, is quite different from the private sector in that it consists of at least three different overlapping social systems or "domains". They are the *political*, the *managerial* and the *service* domain. Each has different ways of seeing the world, adopts different techniques for getting work done and requires different personnel practices. So just as professionals and specialists cannot understand the primacy of management, many managers cannot understand politicians and policy–makers. There are two key issues: strategies, approaches and techniques appropriate to the private sector should not be simply transferred to the public sector; and approaches and techniques from one domain should not be implemented in another. One domain's solution can become another domain's problem[8].

Parston, in a discussion of public sector management, has also identified a number of related obstacles that make public management practice both difficult to define and possibly more complex than private sector management:

i) in line with traditional distinctions between policy–making and public administration, public sector managers are seen to have little role in determining *why* their organisations exist and hence in explicating what values they intend to create; this distinction maintains that the public manager's role should focus on operations and on some aspects of strategy, but not on formulation of policy or mission;

ii) the means of holding managers accountable (in a mutually agreed fashion) for achievement of non–financial performance are limited and arguable. (How is a manager's achievement of equity objectives to be assessed?). As a consequence, most systems of managerial accountability are reduced to using known, quantitative financial measures, implying a primacy of economic value and performance which might not be the primary objective of the public sector organisation;

iii) there are few if any incentives in public sector organisations to encourage managers to act more like entrepreneurs in pursuing the creation of value or the achievement of objectives, however expressed. This frequently results in an aversion to risk–taking, the stifling of innovation, and a type of management practice often characterised by charges that public sector managers "keep their heads down" or "cover their backs" — i.e. follow prescribed administrative procedures rather than act as managers;

iv) although organisational boundaries of managerial responsibility are often un-clear and overlapping, managers frequently are allowed little discretion in ne-gotiating local inter–organisational responsibilities and practices;

v) the conflicting requirements of annual budgetary constraints and the short–term political agenda versus long–term planning can encourage managers to focus on short–term performance as a measure of success. This in turn can frequently result in failure to adhere to long–term objectives, thus reducing planning to an unreal and unhelpful but intensely time–consuming managerial exercise;

vi) there is a general lack of support for a leadership ethos among public sector managers, which is maintained by a political reluctance to underwrite entrepreneurial behaviour and the management of risk. Coming full circle, this lack of leadership sustains the conception of the public manager as someone who has little role in the determination of organisational policy or mission[9].

The obstacles described by Parston and the complexity of the different "domains" suggest that public sector managers require something rather different from the models prescribed for their private sector counterparts. Little work has been done in this area[10] and much of the recent developmental work does not examine critically what defines public sector management.

In moves towards greater flexibility in personnel policy and practice, we need to be clear about the approach being taken. Whose assumptions, whose objectives, whose definition of success are they legitimising: those of the private sector or public sector and, if public sector, how is it being defined?

Managerial Delegation and Decentralisation

The first point is that there is a crucial distinction to be made between the term managerial delegation or devolution and functional and/or spatial decentralisation. In this paper the focus has been on managerial delegation rather than functional and spatial decentralisation.

We have witnessed increasing attempts to delegate more responsibility to manag-ers, starting with financial management changes, followed by personnel management changes. However, although it is often argued that managers want and need the "space to manage", practice does not always conform with this argument. A number of issues are raised by this tension. First, do managers want to manage? In countries with managerial cultures, managers generally do want to manage and *have* to manage; in other traditions and cultures, this is not necessarily the case. There seem to be some differences between senior managers and middle level managers. Senior manag-ers are increasingly defining their role as management and want the necessary respon-sibilities and authority, including personnel management functions. Middle level man-agers, who are often professionals and specialists working at an operational level, seem less attracted by these managerial responsibilities, many seeing them as a necessary chore. This ambivalence on the part of some managers can leave personnel managers, whether located centrally or in departments, in a difficult position in terms of author-ity, responsibility and influence.

The second issue involves the role of the personnel staff. In a system with mana-gerial delegation, what becomes of the personnel role? Many personnel managers are struggling to cope with new roles and with the loss that giving up traditional roles implies. The new roles arguably include a more strategic policy approach, information and records management, monitoring, protesting individual rights, counselling and consultancy. Yet it is unclear how much attention has been given to defining and supporting the functioning of these new roles, for example through training, and whether they are accepted by both line managers and personnel staff alike.

Issues of dependency and counter-dependency seem to continue, with neither managers nor personnel staff clear about their new roles and responsibilities.

A third issue, and an important one, concerns the effect of the development of both increased managerial responsibility on overall direction and control from the centre, and of political accountability. There is obviously considerable scope for clashes between the needs of these two legitimate policy directions. From my own managerial experience in Australia and comparative work in Sweden and the UK, it appears that countries oscillate between the two extremes. As the UK encourages more management and financial responsibility and accountability through the chief executives of the new "Next Steps" agencies, the Swedish government is concerned that the Directors-general of their agencies need to be brought under more political and financial control.

Managers and Management

The move towards more flexible personnel policies and practice implies that managers become personnel managers (as well as, for example, financial managers). The definition and scope of management and the skills required of managers are therefore expanding. Let us briefly review some of the issues facing senior managers in implementing flexible personnel policies. They include the following:

— the culture of management and performance may not be shared by lower level managers and professionals and specialists;
— the new culture of management may appear threatening to more traditionally trained and experienced managers;
— resistance from, or insecurity on the part of, staff may threaten to undermine managers' authority;
— there may be anxieties about performance and non-performance or about the rise of competition rather than co-operation in performance management systems;
— the apparent withdrawal of traditional frameworks, rules and methods may give rise to uncertainty and anxiety over spans of control;
— some staff may be confused about the new routes to career progress;
— managers are having to work with changing organisational forms (e.g. task forces, idea groups, implementation teams) as well as more defined work groups;
— the necessary central support may be lacking if central agencies and services have not worked out their new roles;
— the variety of staff contracts (tenured, contract, full-time, part-time) may pose problems in relation to work planning/programming and progress, and in terms of developing new organisational cultures, strong motivation and high morale;
— differences between political, managerial and service domains may require managers to perform a variety of sometimes conflicting roles;

— there may be clashes between political objectives and direction and delegated managerial authority.

These issues which have to be addressed imply that considerable training and retraining is needed for managers and personnel staff at all levels. It remains to be seen whether the funds to support these needs will be available, although a number of countries have made considerable progress in this regard.

Distributional Effects

The question of who benefits from more flexible personnel policies needs to be addressed. First, however, we need to clarify whether moves towards more flexible personnel management systems involve an overarching strategic shift or whether in reality little has changed so far. Atkinson and Meager in a report on the implementation of the "Flexible Firm" in the UK note that: "Although the observed changes were widespread, they did not cut very deeply in most firms, and therefore the outcome was more likely to be marginal, ad hoc and tentative rather than a purposeful and strategic thrust to achieve flexibility"[11]. Is this also true in the public service? Clearly there have been many proposed changes across OECD countries and the flexibility issue is under discussion almost everywhere, but just how much has been achieved and who has benefited needs to be studied systematically. This set of papers deals mainly with senior managers and we have seen many changes to their working conditions, responsibilities, contracts, pay and accountabilities. For many at this level there do seem to be benefits, although "permanence" may no longer be one of them. The evidence further down the hierarchy is less clear and further research is needed. A number of studies and surveys have been completed in the UK in the private sector on this issue and similar approaches should be pursued for the public service.

In addition, it may be useful to examine further the impact of flexible personnel policies in relation to equal opportunity policies and practices. For some, the increased flexibility through part–time work and flexible working hours is beneficial, although this may be offset through moves towards greater flexibility which may include short–term contract employment instead of permanent contracts. We should perhaps ask ourselves whether flexible personnel policies are a new response to the changing needs of public service employees or whether they are merely an employer–led repackaging of old employment practices.

The Inter–relationship of Reforms

The final issue involves the inter–relationship of different reforms, and in particular the interaction of financial and personnel reforms. Put simply, the successful implementation of personnel management reforms calls for considerable financial, managerial and political support and commitment. It also requires a longer–term perspective, as many of the changes can only be achieved with the reinforcement of attitudinal and cultural change in organisations as a whole. It is unclear from the evidence whether sufficient support is available. For example, crucial training and retraining programmes have been cut or postponed in some cases; investment in developing a capacity to deal with the complexities of organisational change has not always been made; and the understanding of change often appears to be seen in terms of "quick fix" solutions rather than longer–term cultural change.

Conclusion

This paper has given selective coverage to a number of issues that have arisen from the introduction by OECD governments of initiatives to achieve more flexibility in personnel policy and practice. It has been argued that some governments are seeking to transform their administrations from an administrative culture to a managerial culture. This is being carried out alongside public expenditure restraint policies and moves towards modernisation and reform. The private sector has been influential as the source of many of the ideas and business methods taken up by the public service, but it has itself also been under pressure to modernise in the light of increasing international competition.

As we near the end of the decade, we might speculate on what is to be confronted in the 1990s. Governing in the post–industrial world may involve continuing pressure to perform more efficiently with fewer people, further public expenditure restraint, increasing decentralisation, increasing central political control, more flexibility in personnel policy and practice, potential weakening of individual and democratic rights, expanding consumer interest and power, new public service organisational forms and relationships, further changes to the role of the State, less sovereignty for nation states in an increasingly internationalised world. We could go on. Many of these developments are contradictory and will cause tensions, impose limits and generate trade–offs in relation to public management activity.

In thinking about strategies for responding to these challenges, there are a number of areas which could benefit from international sharing of innovation and experience. These include, for example, further exploration and evaluation of public management ideas and practices; further examination of how flexible personnel management systems can be developed, the implications of the changes which are taking place and the new roles and skills required of personnel managers in the public service; analysis of reform objectives, methods of managing change and management development and training needs; and exploration of new policy, organisational and political skills required for governing in a rapidly changing and increasingly internationalised world.

NOTES AND REFERENCES

1. OECD, *Flexibility in the Labour Market*, Paris: 1986.

2. Pollert, A. "The 'Flexible Firm', Fixation or Fact?", *Work Employment and Society*, September (1988), pp. 280–316.

3. Deakin, S. "Labour Law and the Developing Employment Relationship in the UK", *Cambridge Journal of Economics*, 10 (1986), pp. 225–246; Lewis, J. "The Changing Structure of the Workforce", paper presented to a conference on "Change at Work and Flexibility", Northern College, March 1987.

4. Wilkinson, F. (ed.), *The Dynamics of Labour Market Segmentation*, London: Academic Press, 1981.

5. Atkinson, J. "Manpower Strategies for Flexible Organisations", *Personnel Management*, August 1984; *Flexibility, Uncertainty and Manpower Management*, IMS Report, N° 89, Brighton, Institute of Manpower Studies, 1985.

6. Nichols, T. *The British Worker Question*, London: Routledge and Kegan Paul, 1986.

7. Perry, J.L. and Kraemer, K.L. (eds.), *Public Management: Public and Private Perspectives*, California: Mayfield Publishing Co., 1983.

8. Hoggett, P. Private communication, School for Advanced Urban Studies, University of Bristol, 1988.

9. Parston, G. "Public Sector Management Initiative", mimeo, King's Fund College, London, 1988.

10. Kooiman, J. and Eliassen, K.A. *Managing Public Organisations*, London: Sage, 1987; Local Government Training Board, *Management in the Public Domain — A Discussion Paper*, Luton: Local Government Training Board, 1988; Metcalfe, L. and Richards, S. *Improving Public Management*, London: Sage, 1987; Moore, M.H. "A Conception of Public Management", mimeo, Harvard University, 1983.

11. Atkinson, J. and Meager, N. "Is 'Flexibility' Just a Flash in the Pan?", *Personnel Management*, September 1986.

WHERE TO OBTAIN OECD PUBLICATIONS
OÙ OBTENIR LES PUBLICATIONS DE L'OCDE

Argentina – Argentine
Carlos Hirsch S.R.L.
Galeria Güemes, Florida 165, 4° Piso
1333 Buenos Aires
Tel. 30.7122, 331.1787 y 331.2391
Telegram: Hirsch-Baires
Telex: 21112 UAPE-AR. Ref. s/2901
Telefax:(1)331-1787

Australia – Australie
D.A. Book (Aust.) Pty. Ltd.
11–13 Station Street (P.O. Box 163)
Mitcham, Vic. 3132   Tel. (03)873.4411
Telex: AA37911 DA BOOK
Telefax: (03)873.5679

Austria – Autriche
OECD Publications and Information Centre
4 Simrockstrasse
5300 Bonn (Germany)   Tel. (0228)21.60.45
Telex: 8 86300 Bonn
Telefax: (0228)26.11.04
Gerold & Co.
Graben 31
Wien I   Tel. (0222)533.50.14

Belgium – Belgique
Jean De Lannoy
Avenue du Roi 202
B-1060 Bruxelles
Tel. (02)538.51.69/538.08.41
Telex: 63220 Telefax: (02)538.08.41

Canada
Renouf Publishing Company Ltd.
1294 Algoma Road
Ottawa, Ont. K1B 3W8 Tel. (613)741.4333
Telex: 053–4783 Telefax: (613)741.5439
Stores:
61 Sparks Street
Ottawa, Ont. K1P 5R1   Tel. (613)238.8985
211 Yonge Street
Toronto, Ont. M5B 1M4 Tel. (416)363.3171
Federal Publications
165 University Avenue
Toronto, ON M5H 3B9   Tel. (416)581.1552
Telefax: (416)581.1743
Les Publications Fédérales
1185 rue de l'Université
Montréal, PQ H3B 1R7   Tel. (514)954–1633
Les Éditions La Liberté Inc.
3020 Chemin Sainte-Foy
Sainte-Foy, P.Q. G1X 3V6
Tel. (418)658.3763
Telefax: (418)658.3763

Denmark – Danemark
Munksgaard Export and Subscription Service
35, Norre Sogade, P.O. Box 2148
DK-1016 Kobenhavn K
Tel. (45 33)12.85.70
Telex: 19431 MUNKS DK
Telefax: (45 33)12.93.87

Finland – Finlande
Akateeminen Kirjakauppa
Keskuskatu 1, P.O. Box 128
00100 Helsinki   Tel. (358 0)12141
Telex: 125080 Telefax: (358 0)121.4441

France
OECD/OCDE
Mail Orders/Commandes par correspon-
dance:
2 rue André-Pascal
75775 Paris Cedex 16   Tel. (1)45.24.82.00
Bookshop/Librairie:
33, rue Octave-Feuillet
75016 Paris   Tel. (1)45.24.81.67
                            (1)45.24.81.81
Telex: 620 160 OCDE
Telefax: (33-1)45.24.85.00
Librairie de l'Université
12a, rue Nazareth
13602 Aix-en-Provence   Tel. 42.26.18.08

Germany – Allemagne
OECD Publications and Information Centre
4 Simrockstrasse
5300 Bonn   Tel. (0228)21.60.45
Telex: 8 86300 Bonn
Telefax: (0228)26.11.04

Greece – Grèce
Librairie Kauffmann
28 rue du Stade
105 64 Athens   Tel. 322.21.60
Telex: 218187 LIKA Gr

Hong Kong
Government Information Services
Publications (Sales) Office
Information Service Department
No. 1 Battery Path
Central   Tel. (5)23.31.91
Telex: 802.61190

Iceland – Islande
Mal Mog Menning
Laugavegi 18, Postholf 392
121 Reykjavik   Tel. 15199/24240

India – Inde
Oxford Book and Stationery Co.
Scindia House
New Delhi 110001   Tel. 331.5896/5308
Telex: 31 61990 AM IN
Telefax: (11)332.5993
17 Park Street
Calcutta 700016   Tel. 240832

Indonesia – Indonésie
Pdii-Lipi
P.O. Box 269/JKSMG/88
Jakarta12790   Tel. 583467
Telex: 62 875

Ireland – Irlande
TDC Publishers – Library Suppliers
12 North Frederick Street
Dublin 1   Tel. 744835/749677
Telex: 33530 TDCP EI Telefax : 748416

Italy – Italie
Libreria Commissionaria Sansoni
Via Benedetto Fortini, 120/10
Casella Post. 552
50125 Firenze   Tel. (055)645415
Telex: 570466 Telefax: (39.55)641257
Via Bartolini 29
20155 Milano   Tel. 365083
La diffusione delle pubblicazioni OCSE viene
assicurata dalle principali librerie ed anche
da:
Editrice e Libreria Herder
Piazza Montecitorio 120
00186 Roma   Tel. 679.4628
Telex: NATEL I 621427
Libreria Hoepli
Via Hoepli 5
20121 Milano   Tel. 865446
Telex: 31.33.95 Telefax: (39.2)805.2886
Libreria Scientifica
Dott. Lucio de Biasio "Aeiou"
Via Meravigli 16
20123 Milano   Tel. 807679
Telex: 800175

Japan – Japon
OECD Publications and Information Centre
Landic Akasaka Building
2-3-4 Akasaka, Minato-ku
Tokyo 107   Tel. 586.2016
Telefax: (81.3)584.7929

Korea – Corée
Kyobo Book Centre Co. Ltd.
P.O. Box 1658, Kwang Hwa Moon
Seoul   Tel. (REP)730.78.91
Telex: 735.0030

**Malaysia/Singapore –
Malaisie/Singapour**
University of Malaya Co-operative Bookshop
Ltd.
P.O. Box 1127, Jalan Pantai Baru 59100
Kuala Lumpur
Malaysia   Tel. 756.5000/756.5425
Telex: 757.3661
Information Publications Pte. Ltd.
Pei-Fu Industrial Building
24 New Industrial Road No. 02–06
Singapore 1953   Tel. 283.1786/283.1798
Telefax: 284.8875

Netherlands – Pays-Bas
SDU Uitgeverij
Christoffel Plantijnstraat 2
Postbus 20014
2500 EA's-Gravenhage   Tel. (070)78.99.11
Voor bestellingen: Tel. (070)78.98.80
Telex: 32486 stdru Telefax: (070)47.63.51

New Zealand –Nouvelle-Zélande
Government Printing Office
Customer Services
P.O. Box 12–411
Freepost 10–050
Thorndon, Wellington
Tel. 0800 733–406   Telefax: 04 499–1733

Norway – Norvège
Narvesen Info Center – NIC
Bertrand Narvesens vei 2
P.O. Box 6125 Etterstad
0602 Oslo 6
Tel. (02)67.83.10/(02)68.40.20
Telex: 79668 NIC N Telefax: (47 2)68.53.47

Pakistan
Mirza Book Agency
65 Shahrah Quaid-E-Azam
Lahore 3   Tel. 66839
Telex: 44886 UBL PK. Attn: MIRZA BK

Portugal
Livraria Portugal
Rua do Carmo 70–74
1117 Lisboa Codex   Tel. 347.49.82/3/4/5

**Singapore/Malaysia
Singapour/Malaisie**
See "Malaysia/Singapore"
Voir "Malaisie/Singapour"

Spain – Espagne
Mundi-Prensa Libros S.A.
Castello 37, Apartado 1223
Madrid 28001   Tel. (91) 431.33.99
Telex: 49370 MPLI Telefax: (91) 275.39.98
Libreria Internacional AEDOS
Consejo de Ciento 391
08009 –Barcelona   Tel. (93) 301–86–15
Telefax: (93) 317–01–41

Sweden – Suède
Fritzes Fackboksföretaget
Box 16356, S 103 27 STH
Regeringsgatan 12
DS Stockholm   Tel. (08)23.89.00
Telex: 12387 Telefax: (08)20.50.21
Subscription Agency/Abonnements:
Wennergren-Williams AB
Box 30004
104 25 Stockholm   Tel. (08)54.12.00
Telex: 19937 Telefax: (08)50.82.86

Switzerland – Suisse
OECD Publications and Information Centre
4 Simrockstrasse
5300 Bonn (Germany)   Tel. (0228)21.60.45
Telex: 8 86300 Bonn
Telefax: (0228)26.11.04
Librairie Payot
6 rue Grenus
1211 Genève 11   Tel. (022)731.89.50
Telex: 28356
Maditec S.A.
Ch. des Palettes 4
1020 Renens/Lausanne Tel. (021)635.08.65
Telefax: (021)635.07.80
United Nations Bookshop/Librairie des Na-
tions-Unies
Palais des Nations
1211 Genève 10
Tel. (022)734.60.11 (ext. 48.72)
Telex: 289696 (Attn: Sales)
Telefax: (022)733.98.79

Taïwan – Formose
Good Faith Worldwide Int'l. Co. Ltd.
9th Floor, No. 118, Sec. 2
Chung Hsiao E. Road
Taipei   Tel. 391.7396/391.7397
Telefax: (02) 394.9176

Thailand – Thalande
Suksit Siam Co. Ltd.
1715 Rama IV Road, Samyan
Bangkok 5   Tel. 251.1630

Turkey – Turquie
Kültur Yayinlari Is–Türk Ltd. Sti.
Atatürk Bulvari No. 191/Kat. 21
Kavaklidere/Ankara   Tel. 25.07.60
Dolmabahce Cad. No. 29
Besiktas/Istanbul   Tel. 160.71.88
Telex: 43482B

United Kingdom – Royaume-Uni
H.M. Stationery Office
Gen. enquiries   Tel. (01) 873 0011
Postal orders only:
P.O. Box 276, London SW8 5DT
Personal Callers HMSO Bookshop
49 High Holborn, London WC1V 6HB
Telex: 297138 Telefax: 873.8463
Branches at: Belfast, Birmingham, Bristol,
Edinburgh, Manchester

United States – États-Unis
OECD Publications and Information Centre
2001 L Street N.W., Suite 700
Washington, D.C. 20036–4095
Tel. (202)785.6323
Telex: 440245 WASHINGTON D.C.
Telefax: (202)785.0350

Venezuela
Libreria del Este
Avda F. Miranda 52, Aptdo. 60337
Edificio Galipan
Caracas 106
Tel. 951.1705/951.2307/951.1297
Telegram: Libreste Caracas

Yugoslavia – Yougoslavie
Jugoslovenska Knjiga
Knez Mihajlova 2, P.O. Box 36
Beograd   Tel. 621.992
Telex: 12466 jk bgd

Orders and inquiries from countries where
Distributors have not yet been appointed
should be sent to: OECD Publications
Service, 2 rue André-Pascal, 75775 Paris
Cedex 16.
Les commandes provenant de pays où
l'OCDE n'a pas encore désigné de dis-
tributeur devraient être adressées à : OCDE,
Service des Publications, 2, rue André-
Pascal, 75775 Paris Cedex 16.

1/90

OECD PUBLICATIONS, 2, rue André-Pascal, 75775 PARIS CEDEX 16
PRINTED IN FRANCE
(42 90 011) ISBN 92-64-13353-4 - No. 45125 1990